WISDOM'S BLOSSOMS

WISDOM'S BLOSSOMS

TALES OF THE SAINTS OF INDIA

Doug Glener & Sarat Komaragiri

SHAMBHALA
Boston & London
2002

SHAMBHALA PUBLICATIONS, INC.
HORTICULTURAL HALL
300 MASSACHUSETTS AVENUE
BOSTON, MASSACHUSETTS 02115
www.shambhala.com

© 2002 by Doug Glener and Sarat Komaragiri

Page 193 constitutes a continuation of this copyright page.

9 8 7 6 5 4 3 2 1

First Edition

Printed in the United States of America

♾ This edition is printed on acid-free paper that meets the
American National Standards Institute Z39.48 Standard.

Distributed in the United States by Random House, Inc.,
and in Canada by Random House of Canada Ltd.

Artwork by Sandra Shaeffer Gray and Swati Mukerjee

LIBRARY OF CONGRESS CATALOGING-IN-PUBLICATION DATA
Glener, Doug.
Wisdom's blossoms: tales of the saints of India/Doug Glener and
Sarat Komaragiri.
p. cm.
Includes bibliographical references.
ISBN 1-57062-884-X
1. Saints—India. 2. India—Religion. 3. Spiritual life.
I. Komaragiri, Sarat. II. Title.
BL2003 .G64 2002
294'.092'2—dc21
2002005365

DEDICATED TO PARAMAHANSA YOGANANDA,
WHOSE LIFE AND TEACHINGS ARE OUR INSPIRATION.

TABLE OF CONTENTS ॐ

ACKNOWLEDGMENTS

The authors would like to thank:
Our editor and friend, Beth Frankl, for believing in this book. Robert Arnett, for his inspiration, insight, and support throughout the entire project. Sandy Gray and Swati Mukerjee for their beautiful artwork and loving involvement from the beginning.

Lawrence Kaplan, digital artist and friend, for creating the map of India after hours of patient effort.

Vihari Komaragiri for turning his analytical mind on the manuscript and providing invaluable feedback. Beth Glener, Marilynn Glener, Gail Greenblatt, Subhash Kak, Ramarao Komaragiri, Srikant Mallavarapu, and Christopher Tompkins for taking the time to read the manuscript and providing us with so many helpful suggestions. Padmaja Charla for assisting in research, Murthy Kuchibhotla for translating Ramadasu's poems, and Elaine Yoneoka for helping with the initial artwork.

Doug Glener would like to thank:
Sarat, for sharing his India with me, my wife, Beth, for everything and more, my little angel, Gabriella, my mother

for all her love, my father for instilling in me the love of words, Brother Keshavananda and Brother Devananda for their encouragement, Jackie, Jay, Rebecca, Ian, Ellie, Owen, Mike, Bruce, Terence, Matt, Drew, Bill, Dan Yurkofksy, Josh Nathan, Daniel DoAmaral, Bert, Judy, Ruth, Martha, Rich Reitneckt, Andy Oran, Richard Rubenstein and Bill Voelkel for giving me a start as a writer, Bill Gleason sensei, Chris Jordan sensei, Ken Nissen sensei, my friends at Shobu Aikido and the Boston Meditation Group, Adhip, Rita, and Lil Cow.

In memory: Anne Mohrer and Dean Mace.

Sarat Komaragiri would like to thank:
Doug Glener, for this book is more his than mine, Ramarao Komaragiri for guidance and source materials, my brother Vihari for being there, my grandmother Rukmini Kantam and my mother, Suvarchala, for all the stories they told us, Aparna, Murthy, and Padmaja for their support, Linda for being my guardian angel in the United States, Brother Keshavananda for giving us direction for the book, Brother Satyananda for his encouraging words, and the Gang—Paramjit, Manpreet, Anu, Aradhana, Vilas, Jayesh, Kumar, Tanya, and Rishi—for all the memorable times in Boston.

In gratitude: To my parents Ramarao and Suvarchala.

INTRODUCTION ॐ

THE HINDU SAGES DECLARE that our real nature is *sat-chit-ananda*—ever-existing, ever-conscious, ever-new bliss—but our lives often seem anything but that. We are beset with challenges uniquely our own, confronted with problems particular to our age, and swept up by events far larger than ourselves. And yet we must still fight the daily battle of life.

Though the promise of perfect happiness eludes us, we still believe it to be our true state and, knowingly or unknowingly, direct all our actions to its attainment.

Throughout the centuries, men and women of God have wrestled with the riddle of finding lasting joy in an unpredictable world and have discovered perennially useful answers that transcend culture and custom. Having overcome tests and desires common to all, the saints serve as living scriptures that encourage and uplift us.

For those who seek such inspiration, they will find in *Wisdom's Blossoms* twenty-six true stories[1] about individuals who transformed themselves. Buddhists, Hindus, Jains, Sikhs, and Sufis, hermits and householders, the wealthy and the poor, scholars and the illiterate—you will meet in this book a variety of men and women whose religious beliefs are indigenous to India. The diversity of their backgrounds

reveals that truth is universal, that the same spiritual principles underlie all the great religious traditions, and that adherence to them sanctifies one's life.

The Bhagavad-Gita, one of India's greatest scriptures, enu-
merates these eternal qualities. Arjuna, the ideal devotee, asks
his guru Krishna, "What are the traits of the divinely inclined
man?" This is Krishna's answer:

> Fearlessness, purity of heart, perseverance in acquir-
> ing wisdom and in practicing yoga, charity, subjuga-
> tion of the senses, performance of holy rites, study
> of the scriptures, self-discipline, straightforwardness;
>
> Non-injury, truthfulness, freedom from wrath,
> renunciation, peacefulness, non-slanderousness,
> compassion for all creatures, absence of greed, gen-
> tleness, modesty, lack of restlessness;
>
> Radiance of character, forgiveness, patience,
> cleanness, freedom from hate, absence of conceit—
> these qualities are the wealth of a divinely inclined
> person, O Descendant of Bharata (best or most
> excellent descendant of the Bharata dynasty).
>
> [GOD TALKS WITH ARJUNA: THE BHAGAVAD-GITA,
> BY PARAMAHANSA YOGANANDA²]

For each quality in the preceding Gita passage, there is in
Wisdom's Blossoms a corresponding story of a saint who
demonstrated, or struggled to demonstrate, that quality.
Perhaps the tales of the spiritual giants of India will more
quickly help us find the peace and happiness we seek.

How and why this book came about is also worth a brief
mention.

For hundreds of years in India, people in towns and villages would gather together at dusk to listen to *bhagavatars* (devotional singers) narrate and sing stories of saints. I was privileged to attend many of these devotional festivals in my hometown of Rajahmundry. On those special occasions, our neighborhood took on a festive air. Colorful electric lights were strung up, streets were cordoned off, and temporary wooden stages were erected. My family and I would make our way to the banks of the Godavari River to an open-air auditorium and sit spellbound while we listened to some of India's finest stage performers recount the lives of Sankara, Ramanuja, Gopanna, Vemana, and others.

These tales were also passed down within families, as they were in mine, where my grandmother and parents told us many inspiring tales at bedtime. Over the years, I realized these were not mere stories but principles by which to live. Like lamps in the dark, they lighted my way though gloom and confusion as I was growing up, revealing to me that the true purpose of life was to find God.

With the Westernization of India over the past few decades, the bhagavatars and their stories began to disappear. It became clear that it was important to record their tales before they were lost forever.

Following in the spirit of the bhagavatars and their method of storytelling, Doug and I explored the motivations and milieu of the protagonists and have tried to present these seekers of truth not as rarefied beings but as sincere and courageous individuals who struggled to live by their convictions no matter the cost.

Swami Sankara, the great eighth-century monist, wrote, "The company of a saint even for a second has the power to transport us across the ocean of delusion." May the stories of these saints hasten our crossing!

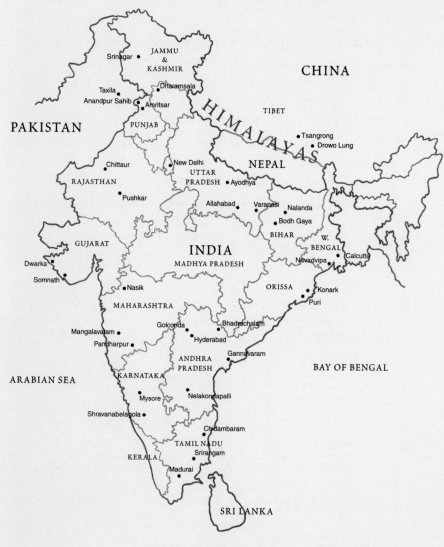

WISDOM'S BLOSSOMS

CHAPTER ONE

Charity

This life is short; the vanities of the world are transient. They only live who live for others. The rest are more dead than alive.

—SWAMI VIVEKANANDA, *THE COMPLETE WORKS OF SWAMI VIVEKANANDA*

UPAGUPTA AND THE COURTESAN ❧

"To those who need help harvesting, I will work in the fields with you. To those who are sick, I will care for you. To those who want to follow the way of the Buddha, let us study the Sutras."[1]

With these words, the wandering monk Upagupta would announce his arrival at every new village he chanced upon. After a few days of living among the men and women of the world, he would set out whither he knew not where, his only companions the sun and the stars.

On this day, Upagupta had walked many miles under a

Upagupta was a Buddhist monk who lived between 100 B.C.E. and 300 C.E. A forest hermit and a renowned preacher in the region of Mathura in Northern India, Upagupta attracted many disciples. The ancient Chinese traveler Hsuan-Tsang brought the story of Upagupta to China, where it spread to the Far East. Two thousand years after his passing, he is still venerated in India and parts of Asia.

scorching sun and at dusk was still far from the nearest town and the hospitality of a charitable stranger. He sought refuge in a shady grove of banyan trees and cooled himself in a stream. As the sun retreated from the heavens, he lay down on a soft patch of grass and fell asleep to a jungle symphony of twittering parrots and monkeys.

The tinkle of anklet bells and the rustle of silk awoke Upagupta from his slumber. Vasavadatta, a beautiful dancing girl, stumbled over him in the gathering twilight. She began to laugh once she could see that she had tripped over a sleeping monk.

All the allures of the flesh were in full bloom in Vasavadatta. Her eyes sparkled with intoxicated youth still untouched by suffering. Raven-black hair cascaded in ringlets down her back. Her skin was as smooth as satin, and her smile was that of one who had drunk deeply of pleasure.

After apologizing for waking him, Vasavadatta said, "Upagupta, I see you wear saffron robes. Please do not tell me that you are a monk who deprives himself of life's delights!"

"It is true," Upagupta chuckled. "I have renounced a home and possessions to find lasting joy."

"What a shame! You are so young and handsome. Do you know that in an instant you will be old and feeble? What then if you haven't found what you are searching for? You will look back at your life and feel bitter for having wasted it in fruitless prayer."

She took his hand and in a rush of excitement continued. "Why don't you come with me to town? Together we can feast and drink and dance. Doesn't that sound more attractive than your fasting and penances?" She wondered if the monk's resolve wavered for a moment.

"Tonight I must meditate," Upagupta firmly replied, although he found her captivating. "For the Buddha says, 'Whoever follows the Dharma is joyful here and joyful there. In both worlds he rejoices.'"[2]

"While you dream of other worlds, I will gladly take what this one has to offer," Vasavadatta said. Smitten by this handsome and resolute man, she excitedly continued, "One last time, Upagupta, please come to town with me!"

"No, not now," he replied with the finality of a man whose mind would not be changed. An inexplicable swell of sadness for Vasavadatta filled him, and he ached to save this carefree butterfly from being caught in the destructive net of desire. "I promise, though, I will come for you another time when you need me."

"Why would I ever need a monk?" said Vasavadatta. And with that, she skipped into the night, leaving a trail of giggles behind her.

Many years had passed since the old monk Upagupta had walked on this same stretch of road. He had come to understand much during his pilgrimages across India. His mind was now unalterably fixed on the Buddha, and when he spoke, his words were suffused with the wisdom of one who knows.

"Ah, I remember this grove of banyan trees!" thought Upagupta. "I had slept here once after traveling all day. And then I was awoken by that young dancing girl."

A mysterious impulse bade him to enter the woods. As he wandered about, he heard the pitiful moans of one in great pain. He hurried toward the cries and found an elderly woman in tattered rags that barely clothed her body. Terrible sores covered her skin. Her hands were shriveled claws. A few stumps were all that were left of her teeth.

"Vasavadatta!" Upagupta exclaimed as he recognized the once-attractive dancing girl. Her beauty had long ago fled with the arrival of disease.

In the same stream in which Upagupta had cooled himself on that hot summer day many years ago, he now washed Vasavadatta. Placing her head in his lap, he stroked her brittle hair.

"All my lovers have deceived me with false declarations of affection. Now everyone despises me. I have led a very evil life." Vasavadatta stared into the monk's calm eyes as she tried to remember his dimly familiar features. "How is it that you have taken pity on me? I deserve contempt, not compassion. Are you the Buddha Himself? You must be, because none other would help such an ugly old creature."

"You need to rest now. Be quiet."

"Who are you?" Vasavadatta pleaded between sobs. It had been many years since anyone had shown her even the smallest kindness.

"I am Upagupta, your friend," the old monk said, all tenderness. "Do you remember me? You asked me to go with you to town, and I promised that I would come for you later. Now I am here.

"Though the world has forsaken you and desire has betrayed you, the Buddha in his unending compassion will be with you life after life until you complete your sojourn on the muddy and treacherous road of illusion."[3]

THE BODHISATTVA

Representation of Padmapani Bodhisattva from the cave paintings at Ajanta, 200 B.C.E. approximately.

In early Buddhism, the term *Bodhisattva* was used to refer to the Buddha before he attained supreme enlightenment. Later on, it was used for any being destined for enlightenment but who chose not to leave the rounds of birth and death in order to help all beings achieve liberation.

Padmapani (literally, "lotus bearer"), also known as Avalokitesvara, the Bodhisattva of compassion, is one of the chief figures in Mahayana Buddhism and is worshiped along with the Gautama Buddha.

CHAPTER TWO

Radiance of Character

The best way to find yourself is to lose yourself in the service of others.

—MAHATMA GANDHI, *GANDHI*

SITAMMA FEEDS
THE POOR ❧

Everyone in Andhra Pradesh knew Dokka Sitamma, and everyone had an opinion about the elderly widow. To the superstitious, Sitamma was an omen of bad luck because she, like all widows, was responsible for the death of her husband. To those blinded by caste and custom, she was an impudent

---

Dokka Sitamma (1841–1909 C.E.) was considered to be a saint during her own life. Inspired by the ancient Vedic dictum, "The guest is God," she spent her days feeding the poor and sick in the village of Lankala Gannavaram.

In the coastal districts of Konaseema, where the many tributaries of the Godavari flow into the Bay of Bengal, her stories are still told today. These tales recount how, after eating food from Sitamma's hands, people rid themselves of bad habits and how some, whose hearts were darkened with jealousy and hatred, were healed.

In a rare honor, King Emperor Edward VII, who reigned over Britain and its Indian colonies (1901–1910), unveiled a portrait of the inimitable philanthropist in the Royal Court in London on his coronation anniversary on January 1, 1903. On that occasion, Sitamma was lauded throughout India as "Apara Annapurna"—an incarnation of the goddess Annapurna. A portrait of Sitamma still hangs on a wall of the famous Annapurna temple in Varanasi.

old woman for refusing to remain confined to her house as a Brahmin widow should. But to the destitute and the devout, Sitamma was mercy personified, for she unfailingly fed the hungry.

With no children of her own to care for and a heart overflowing with motherly love, Sitamma adopted the poor as her sons and daughters. "This illiterate fool is doing great harm by inviting those of a lower station into her home," sniffed the orthodox Brahmins at Sitamma's philanthropy, and when their condemnation failed to deter her, they tried to humiliate her. Though their calumnies and threats stung her, in the end they were little to one whose heart sung of compassion and love.

"Come in! Come in! I have just finished cooking and was hoping that you would join me for dinner tonight." Sitamma would quickly say this to those who came to her in need, thus sparing them the humiliation of having to beg for food.

Because of the chicanery of unscrupulous neighbors who despised her ministry and prized her fertile fields, she found her large holdings reduced year after year, until she was left with only a small plot of land. A famine came, and still Sitamma never turned away those in need, somehow managing to make her shrinking supplies feed a growing stream of hungry souls. Even when she had little to eat herself, she remained grateful for the opportunity to serve, for it gave her great joy, and feeding the poor was her chosen path to salvation.

One night after working in the kitchen for many hours, Sitamma thought, "I have served for four decades, and now my body is worn out. I am nearing the end of my life. It is time for me to go to Varanasi.[1] There I may pass away in peace with the Lord's name on my lips."

For the last few years, Sitamma had dreamed of going to the holy city, for to die there was to be assured of liberation. Every time she set out, however, a desperate beggar or a traveling pilgrim prevented her from leaving. So she would return to her cooking and chanting, putting aside the only desire she had for herself, a desire that daily grew more powerful. But tonight she knew that the hours of her life were few and that only a handful of tomorrows remained.

When morning came, Sitamma gave away her last few possessions so as to bring her charitable works to a close. She hired a bullock cart for the first leg of her journey and set out for Varanasi. Though every rut and rock in the road jarred her old bones and the sun beat on her mercilessly, Sitamma was filled with a happiness that increased with each passing mile, for every turn of the bullock cart's wheels brought her nearer to the end of her earthly sojourn.

At eventide, Sitamma and the bullock cart driver took shelter in a free roadside inn for traveling pilgrims. The hard day of travel weighed on her, and she wearily lied down on a bed of rags. As she began to fall asleep, she was awakened by the cries of young children in the next room.

"I know that you haven't eaten today, but we don't have any food to give you, my love," she heard a father's voice consoling his daughter.

"Can't you ask for some? I'm hungry, and my stomach hurts."

"It's not fit for us to beg. It would be better to starve. But don't worry. Tomorrow we will go to the home of Sitamma. She never sends away those who are hungry."

"Why is Sitamma the only one we can ask?"

"Because she treats her guests with respect and never expects anything in return for her charity."

Once the family had fallen asleep, Sitamma began to stir. "Get up, get up!" she whispered to the snoring cart driver. "We must leave right away!"

"What is the rush? If you have waited for forty years to go Varanasi, you can surely wait one more day," the driver replied sleepily. "We can't travel at night anyway. The road is filled with bandits and wild animals."

"I cannot wait," Sitamma firmly replied.

"Grandmother, do you want to die in a ditch tonight or die in Varanasi in a week?"

"Get up this instant! I have paid you to drive me, and we are leaving now!" And with that, the two travelers set out into the night.

With the first rays of dawn, the starving family awoke and started traveling in the direction of Sitamma's village, un-aware that the one they were looking for had been lying but a few feet away.

The family traveled the same rough and wild roads. The whole way the children cried with hunger, their mother and father struggling to soothe them despite their own wretched condition. By evening they reached Sitamma's village, and after a few inquiries found the dirt path that led to her home.

Seeing the darkened little house, the father despaired. "Is that a light in the window, or is it the reflection of the moon? Do I hear the clanging of a pot, or is that the sound of a cowbell?"

The mother fretted, "She's not home. If she is, will she receive us? Have we come all this way for my children to die of hunger?"

Before the father could knock on the door and end the family's suspense, it swung open. The fragrant smells of dal and rice greeted them.

"Come in! Come in! I have just finished cooking and was hoping that you would join me tonight," Sitamma said cheerfully.

If they had not tried to conceal their tears of gratitude, the family might have observed that Sitamma's sari was frayed and sullied from the dust of the road. If they were not so fatigued, they might have noticed that Sitamma was trembling with exhaustion from being bounced and bruised in the bullock cart and from having to hastily cook this meal. If they were not so hungry, the family might have seen that Sitamma's cupboard and garden were bare and that she had taken upon herself the shame of begging from her neighbors so that they could eat. Sitamma did not die in Varanasi. It was reported, however, that upon her death a great light burst forth from the roof of her house and shot up into the heavens.

GODDESS ANNAPURNA DEVI

Annapurna (literally, "one who has control of food") is the famed consort of Lord Viswanath of Varanasi. Symbolically, she is the mother who feeds all, and is often depicted with a pot of cooked rice, a ladle, and a smile on her lips.

CHAPTER THREE

Fearlessness

A faith is gained as strength only when people are willing to lay down their lives for it.

—MAHATMA GANDHI, *GANDHI*

TEGH BAHADUR HELPS HIS HINDU BROTHERS

"We have come to see Tegh Bahadur on an urgent matter," Pandit Kirpa Ram Datt, the leader of a delegation of Hindu priests, anxiously spoke to a Sikh guard. "Kind Sir, please tell your guru that we request an audience with him."

"Wait here, and I will ask my master if he will see you," the guard replied, wondering what could have caused this group of elderly priests to make the long and dangerous journey

---

Tegh Bahadur (1621–1675 C.E.) was the ninth in a line of ten enlightened Sikh masters. Born to Guru Hargobind (the sixth guru), Tegh Bahadur received training in the arts of warfare and spiritual studies. A warrior, householder, teacher, diplomat, and philanthropist, he was deeply involved in the affairs of the world and admired for his charitable efforts.

In addition to his considerable travels across India as a teacher and his legendary renunciation (Tegh means "renunciation"), he is also remembered for building wells and setting up community kitchens for the poor—good works still practiced by Sikhs today.

from their home in Kashmir to the seat of Sikh power in the city of Anandpur Sahib.

As the guard disappeared into the compound, Pandit Kirpa Ram Datt cast a prayer heavenward, for Tegh Bahadur was their last hope.

"He will see you," said the guard returning, and led the delegation into the guru's private quarters.

"Welcome, My Brothers. Pandit Kirpa Ram Datt! It is good to see you again. What brings you to Anandpur Sahib?"

Regal in bearing and calm in demeanor, the guru of the Sikhs was a lion of a man. With an aquiline nose, a noble forehead, and majestic eyes, his chiseled face expressed an adamantine will. Though over fifty years of age, he retained a youthful vigor that came from a life devoted to austerities and the practice of swordsmanship. A man who was his own master, he had conquered many outer and inner foes.

"The depredations of Aurangzeb grow worse by the day." Pandit Kirpa Ram Datt sounded defeated. Little more needed to be said about the Muslim emperor Aurangzeb, for he was notorious for his many atrocities, among them the killing of his brothers and the imprisonment of his father so he could usurp the throne. Since his ascension, he had stripped his Hindu subjects of their religious freedoms and property rights, and then decreed that their temples, schools, and statues be destroyed.[1]

"Aurangzeb has given us an ultimatum: Convert to Islam or die." Pandit Kirpa Ram Datt struggled to conceal his fear. "You are revered throughout the country for protecting all those who ask for help. It is our hour of need, and there is no one else to whom we can turn."

A funereal quiet fell over the group as they considered Aurangzeb's sadistic stroke of logic. If the influential Brahmins of Kashmir, especially Pandit Kirpa Ram Datt, converted to Islam, the rest of India could be easily forced to follow their example. And if the Brahmins, who were the custodians of the Hindu faith, resisted, they could conveniently be put to death.

"I have struggled and campaigned against the fiend for many years." Tegh Bahadur's voice was like thunder. "He now seeks to break the back of our country with this insidious edict."

As he spoke a young boy of nine burst into the room, his peals of laughter breaking the pall that hung over the group. The boy jumped into Tegh Bahadur's lap and threw his arms around his neck.

"Meet my son, Gobind Rai." Tegh Bahadur rubbed his beard against the boy's face, making him squirm with pleasure. Holding his son close to his chest, he pondered. "Aurangzeb cannot touch me in the stronghold of Anandpur Sahib. I could pass my days here unmolested with my family and watch my son grow into manhood. But is this the example I want to set for Gobind Rai? Is this how the leader of the Sikhs should act? A coward shirking his duty! This is an insult to our martial traditions and faith. And what of my friend Pandit Kirpa Ram Datt and the Hindu priests? If this moment passes by in inaction, thousands will perish by Aurangzeb's sword. Oh, Lord! Where lies my duty? To look after my people and perpetuate my religion or fight for the liberty of all of India even though we Sikhs are imperiled."

Treating his son like the young warrior he was, Tegh Bahadur then explained to Gobind Rai why Pandit Kirpa Ram Datt had requested an audience. "This is quite a dilemma. What is your advice, my son?"

"You are braver than Aurangzeb, and I am sure that if you

help these Brahmins, God will look after me," Gobind Rai confidently replied.

What the child said went straight to the father's heart. A soothing balm of peace stilled his inner tumult, and he knew what course of action he had to take. A great power poured through Tegh Bahadur when he spoke next. "The only way that Aurangzeb will understand the futility of his schemes is if one man true to his convictions is willing to lay down his life in resistance and by doing so show that all his brothers are ready to do the same. Pandit Kirpa Datt, you tell Aurangzeb that you will convert to Islam under one condition: He convert me first."

Pandit Kirpa Ram Datt bowed in awe at a man who would dare to defy the merciless tyrant. The delegation then left Anandpur Sahib to convey Tegh Bahadur's challenge to Aurangzeb.

Clouds of foreboding gathered as Tegh Bahadur prepared to travel to Delhi to meet his nemesis. He gave instructions to his disciples that Gobind Rai be installed as the next Sikh guru should he not return.[2] The faith the boy demonstrated the day the Brahmins came made Tegh Bahadur certain that his son would one day be a great leader.

On the eve of his departure, he addressed his flock. "My friends! Today I set out to tell Aurangzeb that all people—Sikhs, Hindus, or Muslims—have the right to pray to God as they see fit. I am ready to go alone on this mission fraught with danger, but I invite any man who feels as I do to come with me."

Three men stepped forward: Mati Das, Dyala, and Sati Das. "We will go with you, Guru, for we believe in this cause."

"Reflect on what I say," Tegh Bahadur said as a final message to his followers. "To not fight for what is right because of self-interest and attachment invites great evil. When we walk through the portals of this life into the next, we go alone to be judged by our deeds. None then can answer for our actions—neither parents, children, nor friends—only ourselves. Unflinchingly adhere to *Dharma*[3] no matter the price, and you will be sanctified."

Under an ashen sky, the Sikh guru and his three trusted companions set out for Delhi. As soon as they left the protected environs of Anandpur Sahib, they were ambushed by a legion of soldiers and brought in chains to the court of the dreaded Mughal emperor.

"So this is the guru of the Sikhs. Bring him to my feet." Aurangzeb walked around his manacled prisoner several times, as if trying to understand the man who had dared to challenge him. "I would like to make you an offer, Bahadur. Convert to Islam, and you shall be a governor with power over vast dominions. Together we can rule over an empire the likes of which the world has yet to see. What do you say?"

"Are you trying to purchase my faith?" Tegh Bahadur responded. "Let us not waste time. You will never convert me to Islam. Accept this truth, and repeal your edict against the Hindus."[4]

"I find your willingness to stand in place of the cowards of Kashmir quite extraordinary. It is a shame, for you could have been an invaluable ally. At any rate, these Hindus sit in front of idols performing ridiculous rituals, yet their gods do not help them. It is a false religion. Do you not agree?" Aurangzeb wanted to draw out the one man who did not fear him.

"I may disagree with a man's beliefs, but I would give my life for his right to pray as he sees fit." The guru looked at the emperor and spoke deliberately. "Only those who have hurt others are the ones who practice a false religion.

The court gasped. Aurangzeb laughed. "I can see why you are the leader of your people. You fearlessly speak your mind. It is said that you are a holy man, too. Perform a miracle for me right now, and I will set you free," Aurangzeb baited.

"Miracles are gifts from God given to those of deep faith. They are not for the curious. If I were to perform one for you on command, I would be no better than a street-corner magician who hawks his tricks for a few rupees. I shall not oblige you."

"How sad!" Aurangzeb's lip curled in contempt. "I ask one last time: Why did you decide to risk your life to help these Hindu pagans?"

"Stop one man from worshiping as he pleases, and it is only a matter of time before we are all in the same bondage. As a son of God, it is my duty to resist this evil."

"Enough of your lectures!" shouted the emperor. "Torture him until he agrees to convert or pleads for death!"

Soldiers pounced on Tegh Bahadur and his followers and dragged them to Kowali prison, a hellish pit from which no one emerged alive. For six days the soldiers subjected them to the most unspeakable tortures until they realized they could break their prisoners' bones but not their spirits. When they ran out of ways to inflict pain, the guards pulled Tegh Bahadur and his companions by the hair and into the street. Before them stood Aurangzeb on a platform with five hooded men.

"Bahadur, I have grown weary waiting for you to convert, so I am going to help you make your decision more quickly." The tyrant's dark eyes were filled with venom. "Bring me the first prisoner! Bahadur! Will you convert to Islam? If you do, I will spare your friend's life."

"Do not ask this of my guru. I would rather die," Mati Das answered.

"Then so be it."

Guards pulled Mati Das to his feet and tied each of his arms to a pole. A hooded executioner descended from the platform with a saw in his hand, its sharp metal teeth glinting in the sunlight. He placed it on Mati Das's head and began to saw him in half. Blood ran down his face, but still the Sikh warrior was silent. A few seconds later, his soul fled his body.

"Bring me the second prisoner," Aurangzeb barked. "Bahadur, will you convert to Islam?"

Before Tegh Bahadur could speak, Dyala mumbled through broken teeth, "I choose death!"

"Throw him into the cauldron!" Aurangzeb ordered.

Three hooded men lifted Dyala up and tossed him into the liquid inferno. Though his skin peeled away, the Sikh warrior did not scream. The clumps of hair and flesh that floated to the surface told that Dyala's life had come to an end.

"Bahadur, there are thousands of ways to kill a man, but there are only two of you left. Bring me the third prisoner!" Aurangzeb fumed. "Answer me quickly, for I grow bored of this tedium: Do you choose to convert, or are you as stupid as your friends?"

"I choose death," Sati Das declared.

Sati Das was wrapped in cotton, which was then ignited by a torch. A horrific blaze leapt toward the sky. Sati Das staggered forward, then sideways, and finally fell to the ground without so much as a sigh.

"Bahadur, you were quite courageous when it was the others' turn to die. Tomorrow we will see if you will be as brave when it is *your* life," Aurangzeb sneered and left.

The guru of the Sikhs was thrown back into the lightless

dungeon. In the dark, the phantasmagoria of the ghastly deaths of his companions played before his eyes. Aurangzeb's taunts that their deaths had been meaningless rent his heart, and he bitterly condemned himself for asking his friends to accompany him to Delhi. A chasm of doubt opened before him, and he agonized if he should have remained in Anandpur Sahib with his wife and son to wage war another day instead of dying a futile death at the hands of such a man as Aurangzeb.

When day dawned and the guards came for Tegh Bahadur, they found him kneeling, rapt in prayer. Sensing an unworldly power in the room, they were afraid to enter, ashamed by their own profanity.

Tegh Bahadur stretched out his hands. "I am ready." The guards bound him and brought him out.

Thousands of people lined the streets. They had come to see if the guru of the Sikhs was willing to give his life for his beliefs and, by his example, inspire all of India with the courage to resist evil.

Unbowed and radiant, Tegh Bahadur strode like a victor to the place of his execution. All who looked into his eyes saw the great light of God burning therein.

"Tegh Bahadur, you stand here today accused of refusing to denounce Sikhism and Hinduism as false religions," the executioner read from a scroll. "However, the emperor Aurangzeb in his great compassion has decided to grant you clemency if you will convert to the true faith of Islam. What say you?"

A hush fell over the crowd as they awaited his answer. Then Tegh Bahadur spoke: "I will give up my head, but will not forsake my faith or those whom I have undertaken to protect."

"People of India, you have heard this man refuse the

emperor's generous pardon," the executioner intoned. "Justice must now run its course."

Tegh Bahadur placed his head on the block. Turning his eyes heavenward, he placed his soul in the safekeeping of the Lord. There came a sickening swoosh, and the ninth guru of the Sikhs was beheaded.

When Pandit Kirpa Ram Datt heard of Tegh Bahadur's martyrdom, he broke down and cried. "Tegh Bahadur! My friend! You have sacrificed your life for our sake. It is a rare man who is willing to die for his own faith. But has there ever been one who forfeited his life for another's?"[5]

CHAPTER FOUR

Cleanness

Cleanness of body and purity of mind is respect for the in-dwelling Taintless Spirit.

—PARAMAHANSA YOGANANDA, *GOD TALKS
WITH ARJUNA: THE BHAGAVAD-GITA*

THE WEAVER, THE FAKIR, AND THE PIG ✌

The fakir[1] Jahangast had grown weary of hearing stories about Kabir, the lowly weaver widely venerated as a saint.

According to the street-corner gossips, Kabir's latest miracle had been the weaving of a cloth so beautiful that it was said to be the handiwork of God. Accounts of how this extraordinary garment radiated a celestial light could be heard

---

"I have stilled my restless mind, and my heart is radiant, for in Thatness I have seen beyond Thatness," sang Kabir (1440?–1518 C.E.), the unlettered Sufi mystic who pierced the veils of delusion. Beloved by Hindus, Muslims, and Sikhs, Kabir stands as one of India's towering spiritual figures. Probably born into a Hindu family, Kabir was orphaned at an early age and was raised by Muslim weavers. His life and teachings have been described as a unique synthesis of Islam and Hinduism, which angered the orthodox of both faiths of his time, but endeared him to the common man. A mark of his universality is that a number of his poems are included in the Sikh holy book, the Guru Granth Sahib.

in every market stall. It was said that even the wealthiest of
Varanasi hesitated to approach Kabir with offers to buy it, believing it was beyond their means.

"I would not care about Kabir and his magic cloth if he did
not perpetrate a number of more serious frauds," Jahangast
said to a friend. With a sour face he went on, "He poses as a
poet, reciting lofty-sounding couplets, but he swindles the innocent by selling ordinary garments at outrageous prices. He
claims to be a renunciant, but he fraternizes with prostitutes
in the guise of reforming them. Most offensive of all is how
he mocks our Hindu brothers for taking stones for gods and
insults us Muslims for turning toward Mecca every time we
pray. Pshaw! A saint indeed!"

"Why be so worried about Kabir? If he is a fake, he will
soon be forgotten like a passing fashion," Jahangast's friend
said, trying to pacify him. "And who knows—what they say
about Kabir might be true. I have heard that he criticizes
only the blind performance of rituals, but he respects all
faiths as true paths to God."

"Please don't tell me that you, too, are becoming an acolyte!
Don't you understand that his teachings are a harbinger of the
end of the world? Before you start garlanding him, I will prove
he is a sham by challenging and defeating him in public debate.
This will reveal to everyone the folly of fawning over a rascal
who spouts a hodgepodge of crackpot beliefs!" Jahangast
scowled.

The fakir was sincere in his righteous indignation. In his
estimation, a person's faith was measured by how scrupulously
he or she adhered to rules and rituals. And here was Kabir
with his mishmash of teachings and maxims that ridiculed the
scholars and the priests, sowing confusion in the minds of the
common folk and causing them to denounce the established

order of things. Proof of this was how his followers had forgotten that the proper station of a weaver was inferior to that
of a fakir, like himself.

Jahangast set out to deliver his challenge, but when he arrived at the home of the weaver, he shuddered in disgust.
The so-called saint was struggling to tie a pig to a doorpost.

"Cleanliness is next to godliness. Yet, this dolt shows his ignorance of this elementary scriptural injunction by keeping
the most unclean of animals at his doorstep," Jahangast smugly
thought and triumphantly turned around. "Discussing the
subtleties of theology with such a buffoon is a waste of breath!
Now to tell the good people of Varanasi about the doings of
this imposter!"

"Fakir! I thought you were coming to challenge me to a
debate. Why are you leaving?" Kabir called after Jahangast.
"Is it because I have tied this pig to the front of my house?"

Jahangast froze, aghast that the weaver was privy to his
thoughts and embarrassed that he had been exposed.

Kabir spoke again, his voice absent of malice. "I may keep
an unclean pig at my doorstep, but you defile your mind with
judgmental thoughts. Which is worse—harboring an intolerant attitude toward a stranger whose approach to God is
different from your own or deliberately violating a hygienic
custom to show an errant brother that there is no room for
condemnation on the spiritual path?"

"What do you mean? An errant and intolerant brother!"
Jahangast tried to sound indignant.

"You pride yourself in being a scholar and a pious man,
but have you forgotten what the Koran says?

And swell not thy cheek
(For pride) at men.

Nor walk in insolence
Through the earth:
For Allah loveth not
Any arrogant boaster.

And be moderate
In thy pace, and lower
Thy voice; for the harshest
Of sounds without doubt
Is the braying of the ass.

[THE KORAN, LUQMAN 31:18–19]

Hearing Kabir quote scripture with a greater insight than his own swept away the last vestiges of Jahanagast's feelings of superiority. Now there was nothing left to do but turn a critical eye upon himself. And he saw that the fault lay not in Kabir's liberal teachings that freely borrowed from several faiths but in his own following of proscriptions while disregarding their spirit.

"I came to defeat you by showing off my learning, but you have bested even me before I have spoken," Jahangast said shamefacedly. "Praise be to Allah! It is clear to me who is the master and who is the student."[2]

CHAPTER FIVE

Compassion for All Creatures

O Arjuna, the best type of yogi is he who feels for others,
whether in grief or pleasure, even as he feels for himself.

—THE BHAGAVAD-GITA 6:32

THE WEDDING FEAST THAT NEVER WAS ∂

It was Prince Arishtanemi's wedding day, and he was filled
with the trepidation that often accompanies the start of a new
chapter in life.

Sitting atop a gaily decked elephant, trailed by a festive procession of family members, Arishtanemi puzzled over how he
was about to be married when he had always dreamed of
roaming the banks of holy rivers as a mendicant. The call of
renunciation had come to him when he witnessed his playmates shoot and kill a dove with an arrow. Watching the bird
in the throes of death, he had suffered as if his own heart had

---

*Arishtanemi, the protagonist in this story, is the twenty-second of twenty-four Jain
tirthankaras (literally, "ford-makers", or liberated masters). Scholarly debate sur-
rounds the dates of his life. Some historians place him between 3000 and 3200
B.C.E. Through his life's example, Arishtanemi helped to further the doctrine of
ahimsa and the spread of vegetarianism in India.*

been pierced, and he resolved never to harm any living thing and to devote himself to attaining liberation.[1]

The desire to be a solitary sage stayed with him throughout his youth, but once he reached manhood, his family told him that his obligation as a prince lay in marrying and siring an heir to the throne. He could not put personal salvation before family duty, and once his mother had formalized the marriage arrangements, he acquiesced.

As Arishtanemi lay in the howdah, the swishing of the elephant's silks lulled him into a daydream, and his thoughts roamed to the years that lay ahead. Rajul, his bride-to-be, was said to be kind, intelligent, and beautiful. Perhaps he would find happiness in the simple charms of conjugal life and forget about the cruelties of the world in his wife's embrace.

A cacophony of crowing and bleating broke Arishtanemi's reverie. Pen after pen of chickens and sheep lined the road, the animals restlessly stirring in their cages.

"What is happening here?" Arishtanemi asked a herder, deeply disturbed by the cries of birds and beasts.

"Haven't you heard that Princess Rajul and Prince Arishtanemi are going to be married today?" the herder replied, not realizing to whom he was speaking. He wore the satisfied grin of a man who had unexpectedly come into a large sum of money. "The guests in the palace are going to enjoy a splendid feast thanks to my animals here!"

"You mean to say that all these creatures are to be butchered for my wedding?" Arishtanemi could feel the animals' anxiety from being hemmed in crowded cages, and he could intuitively sense their fear of death. He watched a lamb bleating for its mother, and in its eyes he saw the fragility and sacredness of life. The thought that it was to be killed for his pleasure filled him with revulsion. It reminded him of the dove's death rattle from many years ago, and once again he felt nauseated.

"Why is no one else disgusted by this?" Arishtanemi thought as he looked at his smiling relatives. "Have we all become so accustomed to the killing of animals that we no longer think it is cruel? And if we are so indifferent to the taking of life, is it any surprise that we go to wars, abandon the sick, and perpetrate innumerable other atrocities? By failing to see the sanctity of life in all creatures, we are unable to see it in each other, and, so blinded by our insensitivity, we march toward our doom."

Suddenly he saw the true nature of the people of his kingdom. If they weren't maneuvering for personal gain or using one another to advance their own petty desires, they were taking up the sword in fits of outright madness. Greed and lust were ever driving them to commit acts of violence in word and deed, and each wrong action bound them more tightly to the wheel of reincarnation and its attendant sufferings.

"Since these animals have been purchased for my wedding feast, I command that you release them from their pens immediately," Arishtanemi ordered the herder.

"What do you mean?"

"You will do as I say, or I will set them free myself!" Arishtanemi climbed down from the elephant. The members of the procession murmured to each other in bewilderment.

"What is going on, my son?" asked Siva Devi, Arishtanemi's mother, as she ran toward him.

"I will not be responsible for the killing of these animals. Their deaths will haunt me for lifetimes! I cannot go on with this wedding."

"You are talking nonsense. We will free the animals, but get back on your elephant and let us continue."

"Mother, I will lose my soul fulfilling kingly responsibilities whose means and ends are brutality and bloodshed. It is better that I leave Rajul right now than go ahead with marriage vows that will bring ruin to us both. My path is not one of a prince but of a renunciant. It is now impossible for me to marry."

"I do not understand you, my son. None of this bothered you yesterday."

"No, these thoughts have always been turning in my mind, but I did not understand their full import until I saw the animals meant for slaughter today. In this hour of my marriage, I finally see what I must do. Just as these birds want to be released from their cages, I want to be released from the bondage of this world. Please let me go."

"What is there for me to say?" Siva Devi stood shocked. "It is madness for me to force a marriage even though your decision will hurt Rajul and bring shame upon our family."

Arishtanemi embraced his mother, wiped away her tears, and began to walk away. He turned to look at her a last time, knowing that one day he would return to help her and all his brothers and sisters cross the ocean of delusion.

BAHUBALI

Standing over fifty-one feet high and carved from a single rock, the statue of Bahubali, also known as *Gomateswara*, remained the world's tallest monolithic carving for many centuries. Built on a hill in Sravanabelagola ("the monk atop the hill") in Karanataka in 981 C.E., it can be seen from a distance of fifteen miles.

This great "sky-clad" Jain saint, whose face shines with serenity, earned renown for standing in one place for so many years that vines grew around his limbs.

CHAPTER SIX

Noninjury

In the presence of a man perfected in ahimsa, enmity in any creature does not arise.

—PATANJALI, YOGA SUTRAS II:35

THE BUDDHA AND THE BANDIT ⁊

In a gloomy forest swamp littered with human bones, the bandit-murderer Angulimala stood poised to plunge his dagger into the chest of his ninety-ninth victim.

"Please don't kill me! Please don't kill me!" shrieked the prisoner, a spice merchant who had braved the haunts of Angulimala in the hopes of transporting his wares to a neighboring town more quickly. But after traveling a few miles into the woods, the diabolical outlaw had pounced upon him, bound his wrists and legs, and dragged him into a forsaken thicket.

The story of Angulimala is so important that Buddhist monks over the centuries have preserved it on numerous stupas, wall paintings, and manuscripts, and, of course, have handed it down as an oral tale. Angulimala was a contemporary of the Buddha (sixth century B.C.E.), and his story is recorded in the holy text of Majjhima Nikaaya 2:86 as the Angulimala Sutta.

"Take my purse! Take my goods! Take whatever you want, but spare my life!" the merchant begged.

"There is only one thing I want: your little finger," hissed the bandit, who had gained notoriety throughout the countryside for chopping off the fingers of his victims and stringing them around his neck, like a garland. He sadistically shook in glee at the merchant's terror, his necklace clacking on his chest in accompaniment.

"If it is only my finger that you want, here—cut it off. But please, let me go." The merchant looked at Angulimala, hoping to elicit compassion, but the monster was all fury and no mercy.

"Shut up, you whimpering coward, and listen to the great Angulimala's matchless accomplishments." The bandit always recited the same soliloquy before killing his victims. Putting a foot on the prostrate merchant's throat, he began his boast. "I was born under a black horoscope that foretold I would be a magnificent murderer. My parents called me Ahimsaka,¹ as if a mere name could undo the writ of the stars. As a child I was obedient and respectful, as a young man studious and philosophical. Just like you, I was desirous of home and hearth and afraid lest they be snatched away from me—in a word, a weakling."

"Yes! Yes! I am a weakling. Have mercy on me, and set me free!"

Angulimala guffawed and stepped harder on the merchant's neck. "I see that you can still talk. Words are something I despise. They are meaningless and idle. Did you know that while at the Gurukula at Taxila,² I loved to debate the question of whether men made their destiny or destiny made men?" Angulimala stroked his matted beard, mocking the gesture of a hoary scholar deep in thought. "My head was stuffed with so much philosophical drivel that my professor was impressed enough to hold a dinner in my honor. I looked forward to being feted. When I arrived at his home that evening, his wife tried to seduce me. I rebuffed her like any gentleman would, and she was so furious she told the professor that I had raped her."

"The stars that were against me from my birth addled the old fool's brain and made him blind to the truth. He believed what his wife said, and insane with anger, demanded that his *Guru-dakshina*[3] be one hundred little fingers from the hands of my victims. The professor hoped that I would meet a quick death by a soldier's sword in attempting to carry out his wishes. Instead, I put my learning to good use to outwit the buffoons who tried to arrest me. I also discovered that killing was rather enjoyable. Thus was born the feared Angulimala. Don't you think I make an excellent villain?"

"You will go to hell for this," cursed the merchant between gasps.

"Where do you think I am? There is no hope for those condemned from birth. All we can do is suffer our fate and take out our misery on those who are happy."

Eyes rolling with madness, breath reeking of death, Angulimala pulled the merchant up to his feet. "It is so nice of you to sacrifice your life for my cause. Only one victim more after you, and I will have completed the Guru-dakshina." Without another word he drove his dagger into his prisoner's heart. As the merchant breathed his last, Angulimala cut off his finger, strung it on his necklace, and left the body to rot in the swamp.

Bounding up the slope, the bandit climbed to an overlook where he could survey the road unseen. Hours passed with no sign of prey, so to amuse himself he counted the dismem-

bered digits of his finger-garland as attentively as a monk
counting prayer beads. When he grew bored with this, he
fretted about what he would do with the rest of his days once
he had achieved his goal of collecting one hundred fingers.

The faint sound of shoes scuffling along the forest path
caused Angulimala to stiffen with excitement. An elderly
woman was making slow progress on the trail. Looking at the
distant figure, he thought she would make for an easy kill.

"Ahimsaka! Ahimsaka!" the old woman started shouting.
"My beloved son! I know that it is you who have become
Angulimala. The king's men are coming for you. Run while
you can. Ahimsaka! Ahimsaka!" Again and again his mother,
Mantani, cried.

Angulimala thought he had obliterated the memory of
Ahimsaka long ago, but hearing his mother's voice in the
wilderness resurrected thoughts of a time when he was still
an innocent. For a fleeting instant, the bandit who feared no
one was a little boy who wanted to put his head in his
mother's lap and cry. His moment of self-pity, however, came
at a great cost, for it opened a floodgate of feelings. The
screams of his victims filled his ears, demons danced in his
skull, and the hunter of men was hunted by his conscience.

"I am not Ahimsaka. I am Angulimala!" Shrieking like a
fiend, he swooped down the slope. His mother would be his
hundredth victim, and then he would continue killing until
he was killed. As he raised his sword to hack off her head, the
two looked at each other: Mantani seeing only her beloved
child, Angulimala seeing his quarry.

"My son! Forgive us! Your father and I did all we could to
outwit your horoscope. We gave you love, shielded you from
all iniquity, and sent you to the Gurukala. Even you had begun
to believe that you could control your destiny until your

teacher ordered you to fulfill that horrible Guru-dakshina! I
know you thought you were doing an honorable thing, but,
alas, my son, you should have refused. A duty is not a true one
if it causes harm. Yours was a misplaced sense of Dhamma."

"There is no such thing as Dhamma."

Just as he was about to strike, he heard twigs crunching behind him. Thinking it was the king's men, he turned around,
but instead he saw a lone monk emerging from the brush.

"Mother, today is your lucky day, for I will spare you and
kill that monk in your place!" Angulimala shouted as a flicker
of mercy fluttered in his dead heart.

"Come back, my son! Do you not know whom you
chase?"

"What do I care? All men quake at the mention of AN-
GU-LI-MA-LA!" He leaped at his newest victim, who, to
his amazement, calmly continued on his way.

"It is futile for you to flee!" Angulimala cackled. Yet, as fast
as he ran, he grew no closer to the monk. "Why prolong your
agony by trying to escape from me? You might as well stop."

"I have stopped, Angulimala." The monk's voice was divine.

"If you think you can confuse me by saying one thing and
doing another, I will hack off all your fingers."

"I have stopped doing harm to all creatures. Now it is time
for you to do the same."

"Who are you?" the bandit whispered, astonished by the
one man who did not fear him. The simple words the monk
had spoken, indisputable and self-evident, resounded with a
power immeasurably greater than his own rage.

"They call me the Buddha, and I have come to help you."

A transcendent compassion flowed from the Enlightened
One's eyes and Angulimala stood hypnotized. Several minutes that seemed like an eternity passed, and in the wordless
exchange a mystical alchemy was wrought deep within him.

He knew that even if he wanted to harm this radiant being, it would be impossible, for the universe would not permit injury to a man perfected in nonviolence.

"Angulimala, you are one of my own. Your temporary veil of delusion has been lifted forever."

As if waking from a nightmare, Angulimala looked about, and for the first time noticed that he stood in a clearing filled with tiny blue flowers. He heard the song of birds and felt the soft earth beneath his feet. A hidden harmony that connected and sustained all life became apparent to him, and he knew that wanton killing was the greatest of sins.

"The madness is gone, and I can now see," Angulimala exclaimed. He collapsed on his hands and knees and wept. "What evil have I done! I have the blood of ninety-nine people on my hands, and I wear their fingers around my neck. Is there no end to my wickedness? Have mercy! Have mercy! Have mercy!" Angulimala screamed as he tore off his finger garland and threw down his sword.

"Be at peace," the Buddha soothingly said. "Let me wash you in the stream. I will make you a monk."

The Buddha and Mantani carried him to the riverbank. When he beheld his reflection in the water, he recoiled at the repugnant image.

"I cannot stand to see myself! The visions in my head! Death would be a merciful release from this agony," Angulimala choked. "There is no hope for me. I am all evil and impurity."

"It is by oneself that evil is done, by oneself that one is afflicted. It is by oneself that evil is not done, by oneself that one is purified. Purity and impurity are individual matters; no one purifies another," the Buddha said.[4] "Angulimala! Awake from the slumber of ignorance. Though your sins be countless, by practice of the Dhamma you shall be freed."

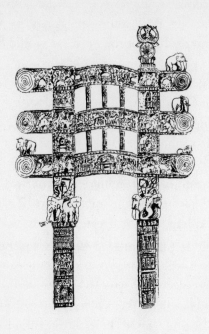

TORANA AT SANCHI STUPA

Representation of the Western *torana* or "decorated gate" at the Sanchi Stupa in Madhya Pradesh. The stupas, monasteries, temples, and pillars at Sanchi date back to the third century B.C.E. and were built by emperor Asoka, who made Buddhism the official state religion of India in 255 B.C.E. The carvings on the *torana* depict scenes from the life of the Buddha.

"Thy mercy is boundless. I will cling to what you say until my last breath."

Wrapping Angulimala in a saffron robe, the Buddha made a monk of the bandit. The novitiate tried to steady himself and tentatively took a step.

As the trio made their way out of the forest, they came upon King Prasenajit and a regiment of his guards. Seeing the Enlightened One, the king climbed down from his horse and reverentially bowed and said, "Beloved Teacher! I have come to capture the one they call Angulimala. Have you heard of his whereabouts?"

"Oh, King! If Angulimala were to stand before you as a monk and in his heart had renounced all evil, what would you say?"

"It would seem easier for the heavens and the earth to exchange their places than for a man so twisted to repent, but if such a stupendous transformation had taken place, it would warrant my clemency," replied the king.

"I now hold you to your word, Prasenajit, for here stands Angulimala." As the Buddha pointed to the monk by his side, the king's soldiers broke rank in terror. "Do not be afraid, for he has pledged to care for the sick and the poor."

"Angulimala, is this true?" the king asked incredulously.

"It is true that I have repented." Angulimala bowed his head remorsefully. "For years I lived a bestial life. Loneliness, hunger, and want were my only companions. I was driven by a bloodlust that was stoked by all the things I was denied by fate—a wife, children, and the little comforts of life. But glory to the Buddha, I am now free of the insanity. The determination with which I tried to fulfill the Guru-dakshina in the past I will now increase a thousandfold to follow the Dhamma. Still, I know I deserve far worse than death and have no right to ask for your mercy. I will not resist if you wish to take my life right now."

Hearing Angulimala's words of contrition, the king turned to the Enlightened One in amazement and spoke. "Buddha Sakya Muni,[5] where my justice could not reach, you have succeeded. The sages have said that the power of love conquers all, and your metamorphosing of this infamous reprobate is proof that all things are possible to the pure of heart." To Angulimala, Prasenajit said, "I had come to hunt you down and kill you. But seeing you so changed, I realize that no man is beyond redemption."[6]

CHAPTER SEVEN

Freedom from Wrath

A sage is content in the knowledge that the Lord is running
the universe and never considers that anything has been done
amiss.

—PARAMAHANSA YOGANANDA, *GOD TALKS*
WITH ARJUNA: THE BHAGAVAD-GITA

THE MAN WHO SPAT
ON A SAINT ✺

"All saints are charlatans, and Eknath is the biggest one of
all!" declared the pundit Ram Pandit[1] to a group of fellow
scholars over dinner. "A conniving beggar, he affects piety to
win alms from the gullible and the simpleminded."

"A cheat!" "A sham!" "A criminal!" cried the diners, each
one envious that the unlettered Eknath had captured the hearts
of the people of Pandharpur, while their academic achieve-
ments had been ignored.

---

*The life of Saint Eknath (1533–1599 C.E.) is held to be the harmonious blend of
householder and devotee. While fulfilling worldly responsibilities, he remained a renunciant at heart, counseling his disciples to forgo unnecessary penances of the body
and to walk a balanced path. Eknath often compared a learned man, bereft of devotion to a prostitute who keeps on changing her ornaments. This theme of useless
and prideful scholarship is a point of interest for the following story.*

"It is indeed an unsolvable mystery that the uneducated choose to see something that is not in a man and refuse to see the real worth of those who are learned, but such are the ways of Kali Yuga!" Ram Pandit wearily concluded.

"A riddle!" "A conundrum!" "Perplexing indeed!"

"I am tired of hearing about Eknath," groused a young scholar, unaware of the unspoken understanding between Ram Pandit and his fellow pundits that they were never expected to act upon their pronouncements. "Does anyone plan to do something about the 'great sage of Pandharpur' other than complain?"

"I intend to!" blurted a blushing Ram Pandit after an awkward pause.

A hush fell over the gathering. Bold action was such a stranger to this group that even the wind and the crickets stopped to listen.

"Ahem, well, ahem," fumbled Ram Pandit as he looked around at his friends' expectant faces. "I have been thinking . . . of a plan . . . that will show everyone once and for all that Eknath is nothing more than an imposter."

"Tell us!" all the pundits cried.

"Tomorrow at dawn, come to the bathing ghat,[2] and you will see for yourself. Once I have unmasked Eknath in front of all, we can bring reason to our deluded townspeople," Ram Pandit improvised, though he had no inkling of what he intended to do.

The next morning found Ram Pandit still without a plan, waiting for his nemesis atop a large rock at the water's edge.

"Here comes Eknath with that silly grin on his face. He acts as if he does not have a worry in the world. I would be just as carefree if everyone in town provided for *my* upkeep," groused Ram Pandit. "He speaks of how earthly things bring only misery, but he always remembers to take his begging bowl!

"Now look at him bathing! Every gesture is done with such affectation and ceremony. See how he closes his eyes to pray but keeps them half open to see if anyone is watching? Well, I am watching you, Eknath, and today, everyone shall see what kind of a man you really are! Where is everyone from last night? I bet those lazy good-for-nothings are asleep in their beds. And here I am with no one to see me in my hour of triumph."

So ran Ram Pandit's thoughts until the sight of Eknath returning from his daily bath interrupted his broodings. Jumping off the rock, Ram Pandit stood before him threateningly. All the gnawing jealousies and frustrations of his life swelled to an uncontrollable pitch, and he spat in Eknath's face.

For a fleeting moment, the peace that filled Eknath's eyes vanished as he tried to understand what had happened. He then smiled at Ram Pandit, turned around, stripped down to his loincloth, and waded back into the river.

"Now what is the fool doing?" Ram Pandit thought as he watched Eknath saying his morning prayers once again. He had hoped Eknath would get enraged, but seeing that it did not happen, he swore, "If he wants to feign patience, let us see how patient he really is."

"Ah, Ram Pandit! Good morning!" yawned one of the pundits from the previous night's dinner. "I wasn't sure if you were serious about what you said yesterday, but here you are! I am filled with anticipation to witness your plan. Have I missed it?"

"No, you have not," snapped Ram Pandit.

"Good, then. Look, here comes Eknath right now!"

As Eknath climbed up the steps, Ram Pandit again jumped off the rock and spat in his face. Once again Eknath turned around and waded back into the river.

"That is quite a plan!" the scholar observed sarcastically.

"I am trying to show that behind his peaceful façade lies an angry man."

"Ah! A very clever stratagem indeed."

The two men sat in an uncomfortable silence until it was broken by the arrival of the rest of their colleagues.

"We rushed here to see you, Ram Pandit!" huffed the pundits. "So Eknath is still bathing. That means we haven't missed anything yet!"

"No, of course not!" Ram Pandit's bravado failed to conceal his discomfiture.

Again Eknath walked up the stairs of the ghat, and again Ram Pandit spat on his face to the disbelief of the onlookers. Just as before, Eknath returned to his morning ablutions.

Over and over this happened, each time more pilgrims gathering to watch, each time Ram Pandit more determined to humiliate Eknath, lest he be humiliated by the failure of his plan. And each time he became more disturbed by the thought, "What if this man is not a charlatan?"

On the hundredth time, Ram Pandit's throat seized, and he struggled for breath. And he knew that he was reaping the consequences of the ninety-nine sins he had just committed.

"Forgive me for what I have done!" cried Ram Pandit, kneeling, his face contorted with pain and remorse. "I set out to prove that you were a fraud by making you lose your temper. But instead I have made a fool of myself before everyone in Pandharpur. Now I know that you are a saint, for who could withstand with such equanimity what I did to you today—not once, not twice, but ninety-nine times? Can you ever forgive me?"

"There is nothing for me to forgive," Eknath said to the prostrate man. "All you did was give me the opportunity to cleanse my sins by taking one hundred dips in the holy Chandrabhaga River."

CHAPTER EIGHT

Peacefulness

Nothing in the affairs of men is worthy of great anxiety.

—PLATO, *TREASURY OF SPIRITUAL WISDOM*

TWO CLOTHS ⁓

"Here comes the whore of God," chortled a street ruffian to his friends as he pointed to Lalleshwari, the devotee who wore nothing more than a beatific smile.

"Did I see you at the brothel last night?" added another, who thought it idiotic that a woman would go naked as a show of her renunciation.

"She's too ugly to find work in a brothel," said a third.

Taunts and insults were not new to Lalleshwari, who was as unconcerned about her nakedness as the orthodox were appalled by it. The stoic demeanor she now evinced was lifetimes removed from the days when she was a sensitive bride filled

---

Lalleshwari (1320–1389 C.E.), also known as Lal Ded and Lalla Yogiswari, is one of the more unusual figures in India's religious history. Born in Kashmir, married at age twelve, Lalleshwari received notoriously harsh treatment at the hands of her mother-in-law. When she turned twenty-six, she renounced all worldly ties to worship Siva.

Although she was illiterate, she expounded the subtlest teachings of Saivism (worship of Siva) in "Lal Vakh" (literally, "the sayings of Lalla"), maxims that are still quoted today. The Sufis claim her as one of their own, as do the Hindus.

with matrimonial hope. The tender moments of her new marriage, however, were short-lived. Lalleshwari's mother-in-law
took an inexplicable hatred toward her and tried to starve her.
When she would not oblige by dying, her mother-in-law
spread rumors that she was an adulteress. Lalleshwari's husband, believing the accusations, dragged her out by her hair
into the marketplace and humiliated her before the townsfolk.

Sitting in the mud, covered with bruises, Lalleshwari knew
then that she had two choices before her: live the rest of her
life as a shamed woman cowed by the opinion of others or
free herself from the tyranny of the ego's endless demands for
respect and recognition. Thus, she decided to follow the ways
of the *digambara*[1] yogis, hermits who wore the sky and the
clouds as their only clothes to destroy pride, shame, and love
of the body.

As Lalleshwari passed by the thugs who had just insulted
her, one of them threw a clod of dirt at her.

"What are you boys doing?" shouted a cloth merchant as
he ran from his shop across the street. "Leave her alone!"

Taking Lalleshwari by the arm, he pulled her into his store
and locked the door. When the merchant looked into her
eyes, he saw there not distress but a mother's compassion for
her misguided children.

"Why do you make life so hard for yourself wandering
around like this?" he blurted, full of concern. "Are you not
ashamed to be seen naked by men? Can't you wear a sari like
every other woman?"

"I refuse to identify myself with this outer garment of flesh
and skin, which must be sloughed off at death. I am in
essence spirit, masquerading as men and women in my different incarnations. So why should I pay heed to that which
is transitory and unreal?" Lalleshwari replied. The merchant

was astonished that she could exude such calm strength after the disturbing encounter.

"What would have happened if I had not saved you a few moments ago from those 'illusory' men?" Though momentarily impressed by Lalleshwari's equanimity, he was still a practical man. "Your philosophical concepts are charming as long as you stay in your cave far from town. But when you are in the company of others, I do not see how you can be so unconcerned with the world."

"There are no half-measures in the spiritual life, my son!" Lalleshwari said. "May I borrow two pieces of cloth from your shop that are equal in weight?"

"Yes, yes, of course!" The shopkeeper was baffled at the strange request.

She unhurriedly draped one cloth over her left shoulder and the second cloth on her right, yet that did little to conceal her nudity.

"I will tie a knot in the cloth on my right each time I meet with praise today. And each time I am scorned, I will tie a knot on the left. When I return in the evening we will see what has come of this experiment," Lalleshwari said and then exited into the street.

The first person she met was a Sufi who had once heard her preach.

"I have never forgotten how you said that we might be a Muslim in this life and a Hindu in the next, but we are forever children of God. With so much misunderstanding and hatred between those of different faiths, we would all do well to listen to your words," he bowed and left.

Lalleshwari tied a knot in the cloth that dangled over her right shoulder, as she prayed, "Lord! Bless this brother."

Then she came upon an elderly woman with her grandchildren in tow. "Shame on you for your indecency!" the old woman hissed as she tried to protect her curious grandchildren by covering their eyes with her hands. Lalleshwari tied a knot in the cloth over her left shoulder and thought, "Lord! Bless this sister."

As she wended her way to the lakeside, she came upon a group of fishermen returning with their morning catch.

"Shoo! Mad woman! Get away from our boats. Don't touch our nets. You will bring us bad luck," they scolded. As she tied a second knot in the left cloth, she prayed, "Lord! Bless these friends."

When she returned to town, Lalleshwari was passing by a house when she heard a woman shout to her husband, "Come back inside! It's that woman. She is an ill omen." And Lalleshwari tied another knot. As she reached the end of the street, she met a devout couple with their newborn child. "Mata Lalleshwari, thank you so much for blessing us last year. We have conceived this child by your grace."

So went her day until she returned to the shopkeeper's store at dusk. He looked pitifully at her, for the cloth on the left shoulder with which she tracked the insults she received was full of knots, while the other had but a few.

"Do you now see that you are widely reviled for your behavior?" The merchant felt vindicated.

"Please bring me a scale," Lalleshwari asked, indifferent to his pronouncement.

"Another strange request from a strange woman!" he thought, but he decided to humor her.

"Could you weigh the two cloths?" she asked.

When he put the cloths on the scale, they still were of equal weight.

"You have judged the manner of my life by the number of

knots in these cloths, as does everyone who has ever lived by the customs of the day. Yet, the scale shows that the cloths are equal in weight though they have changed superficially. I am that unchanging fabric no matter how many knots of praise or blame I receive. Established in the soul I am ever at rest, unaffected by the garments of the various bodies I wear and by the comings and goings of the world."[2]

CHAPTER NINE

Renunciation

When all the desires that surge through the heart are renounced, the mortal becomes immortal.

—THE UPANISHADS

LIKE WATER ON A LOTUS LEAF ↝

Although Sundari Nanda was now a nun, she still clung to the sweet words her suitors had lavished on her when she was a princess:

"The gods surely robbed ninety-nine other women of their comeliness to make one like you."

"Your grace rivals that of a swan's."

"Heavenly nymphs are jealous of your charms."

Dwelling on these memories soothed her vanity, yet left her feeling guilty, for she knew that such thoughts were

---

Nanda (sixth century B.C.E.) was born to King Suddhodana and his second wife, Queen Maha Prajapati Gautami, which made her the half-sister of the Buddha. She later went on to become one of the Buddha's most advanced woman disciples.

Historical records state that she was a woman of unsurpassed beauty and grace, so much so that she was called Rupa-Nanda—"one of delightful form"—and Sundari-Nanda—"beautiful Nanda."

inappropriate for one who had renounced the world to follow the Buddha.

When Nanda had first petitioned to enter the order, the
head sister had warned her that the only reason to become a
nun was the desire for liberation. She nodded her head in a
show of understanding, hoping to hide her real motives,
which were to escape the loneliness of palace life and to be
near her mother, friends, and attendants, who had all become renunciants.

In the quiet of the night after the other nuns had gone to
sleep, Nanda now wept aloud. Though once again in the
company of her loved ones, she pined for the days when she
was the cynosure of the palace. She wished to exchange her
nun's habit for her silks and go back to her old life, but her
pride would not brook failure. Yet, Nanda knew she was un-
prepared to meet the rigors of her vocation and could not remain in the order. And so she was a prisoner of her own
making, trapped in a grim little cell and sentenced to a life of
fasts, penances, and silence.

With neither the joys of her old life nor the spiritual con-
solations of her new one, Nanda lived in a netherworld, sustained by memories of flattering words. How she wished she
had honestly answered the head nun before making such a
weighty commitment!

One morning the head nun said, "The Buddha wishes to
speak with each of the sisters privately about the Four Noble
Truths." One by one, the nuns met with the Enlightened
One. When they left, their eyes glimmered with serenity and
the peace of understanding.

"I cannot face him," Nanda thought as she waited, anxious that the Buddha would know that she wore the
outward garb of a renunciant while remaining inwardly

enamored of her beauty. Fearful of being exposed as a
hypocrite, she avoided the Buddha by busying herself with
trifling chores, fervently praying that this would give the
appearance that her duties prevented an interview. Just
when she thought that her diversionary ruse had succeeded,
a nun approached her.

"The Buddha has asked to see you."

Dreading a reprimand, Nanda sheepishly made her way to
the Enlightened One.

"I am glad you have come," the Buddha said, smiling. "I
have been thinking today of how generous and loving you are.
You have earned much merit through your sacrifice of palace
comforts." The Buddha knew that his sister cherished praise.

Nanda sighed, relieved that he had not found fault with her.

"I think, Sister, that you are still bound by a desire that
keeps you from finding final freedom. May I help you overcome that which keeps you bound to suffering?"

Nanda tentatively nodded, reluctant to forsake her attachment to her beauty, afraid that the remedy might be
painful. Then the Buddha leaned forward and tapped her
on the forehead.

Suddenly Nanda beheld the most ravishing woman she
had ever seen. So dazzling was the figure that Nanda felt
plain in comparison. If this image of loveliness had been at
the court, Nanda knew she would have gone unnoticed. She
was instantly filled with jealousy at the sight of one who was
more attractive than she.

In the vision, Nanda saw the decades pass in seconds, and
the beautiful woman began to age. Her flesh lost its vitality and
sagged, her lustrous hair became gray and unkempt, and her
dewy skin turned dry and leathery. The millstone of time re-
lentlessly ground on, and before Nanda's eyes, the statuesque

creature wilted into a stooped crone, finally falling lifeless to the ground to become the food of maggots.

Nanda shook at the ghastly vision. "Not me! Please, not me!" she wailed.

"Since this is the fate of all living things, is it not madness to be attached to that which must inevitably decay and die?" the Buddha asked Nanda. "Everyone but the wise is similarly deluded, be it by flattering words, fame, money, or outward appearances. Do not judge yourself too harshly, for this failing is common to all, but strive to remember that everything in this world is impermanent and that the only refuge lies within. Meditate on the truth of these words, and you will be free from all delusion."

Reeling from the experience, Nanda teetered back to the company of her sisters. And the next time she remembered the words of her suitors of years ago, they seemed no more appealing to her than the chattering of monkeys.

THE BUDDHA

Often depicted sitting in the lotus posture, the Lord Buddha's image expresses serene quiescence, while the perfect proportions of his gracious physical form mirror an inner perfection.

The gestures of the hands, called *mudras*, are symbolic. In this picture, the raised right hand and the tip of the forefinger touching the thumb is the *Vitarka mudra*, which stands for the conveying of knowledge through a sermon.

CHAPTER TEN

Purity of Heart

Blessed are the pure in heart: for they shall see God.
—MATTHEW 5:8, THE BIBLE

TO THE LOVER THOU ART LOVE

As the evening stars rubbed their eyes and woke up from their diurnal slumber, King Lakshmana and his entourage gathered in the palace courtyard to hear the nightly reading by the poet Jayadeva.

Excited whispers were exchanged until the arrival of the bard. A handsome man with soft eyes, full beard, and noble carriage, Jayadeva prostrated himself before a statue of Radha and Krishna that had been placed under the spreading branches of an ancient peepul tree.

The story of Jayadeva and Padmavati (twelfth century C.E.) is considered by many in India to be the epitome of a spiritual marriage. Jayadeva is remembered for his poem, the Gitagovinda *(Song of the Cowherd), which recounts the love between Krishna and Radha. His Sanskrit songs are also an important part of the devotional music of Orissa, Bengal, and South India. Many of his songs end with the refrain "Jaya Jayadeva Hare," indicating that he had no existence outside of Hari (the Lord as Krishna).*

Turning toward the monarch and the audience, Jayadeva said, "Tonight I will read sections from the *Gitagovinda*. The first four stanzas are Radha's yearning for Krishna, and the last two are Krishna's love for Radha."[1] As he began to sing, his melodious voice enthralled the audience.

Her eyes shed tears everywhere
Like dew from lotuses with broken stems.
Krishna, Radha suffers in your desertion.

Her eyes see a couch of tender shoots,
But she imagines a ritual bed of flames.
Krishna, Radha suffers in your desertion.

She presses her palm against her cheek,
Wan as a crescent moon in the evening.
Krishna, Radha suffers in your desertion.

If you feel sympathy, Krishna,
Play godly healer! Or death may take her.

Cool moon rays scorch him,
Threatening death.
Love's arrow falls.
And he laments his weakness.
Wildflower-garlanded Krishna
Suffers in your desertion, friend.

Bees swarm, buzzing sounds of love,
Making him cover his ears.
Your neglect affects his heart,

Inflicting pain night after night.
Wildflower-garlanded Krishna
Suffers in your desertion, friend.[2]

"The duties of the throne weigh heavily upon me, but
hearing you sing of Radha and Krishna, I remember that my
responsibilities as a king are ephemeral, and it is not the dis-
pensing of justice but the giving of unselfish love that is the
highest virtue." King Lakshmana sighed. "Jayadeva, you have
made me very happy tonight. Name your wish, and it shall
be granted."

"Your Majesty, it has been three months since I left my
home in Navadvipa to come to your court. Though you
have treated me most graciously, I must confess that I miss
my wife, Padmavati. Without her by my side, I feel incom-
plete," Jayadeva answered.

"Say no more. I will immediately send a palanquin with an
escort for her." King Lakshmana was only too happy to grant
this request, for he was uplifted by the poet's companionship
and did not want him to leave the palace. Rumors were also
whispered that Jayadeva had been a wandering ascetic until
he met a seer who had instructed him to marry, so the king
was curious to meet the woman who had turned a renunciant into a pining husband.

Padmavati arrived at the court, and when King Lakshmana
saw the poet and his wife together for the first time, he
thought, "This is what it means to be joined in holy marriage." It was as if the two shared one common soul. By a
mere glance they could communicate their innermost
thoughts, and when they did speak, their words were sweet
and mild, appreciative of the gift they had been given in each
other. Though they took obvious pleasure in each other's

company, theirs was not a narrow love but included the happiness of all. Guileless and sincere, they seemed like two children walking hand in hand back to God.

The king delighted to pass his time with them and showed his affection with little tokens of gratitude, and he wished his own marriage were as harmonious.

The queen and her coterie, however, had a rather different opinion of Padmavati. According to them, she was coarse and stupid but somehow shrewd enough to have seduced Jayadeva, the most charming and handsome man in India. What infuriated the queen most, though, was her conviction that Padmavati had won her husband's affections and was using him to further her own ignoble ends.

And so the royal house split into two warring camps: admirers and detractors of Padmavati. The queen, appointing herself guardian of palace morality, announced that it was her duty to unmask Padmavati before the naive King Lakshmana fell prey to her charms.

"What is love?" A lady-in-waiting, with great artifice, asked this question of the queen's court one day. Jayadeva's inspired compositions sung at twilight had made romance the favorite topic of conversation.

"A thrill of the heart," gushed one.

"A pretty face that speaks little," said another.

"The foolish musings of one who has never been married," offered a third, who, like all the others, was enamored with Jayadeva and secretly jealous of the flawless love between the poet and his wife.

Titters of laughter filled the room as Padmavati forced a

polite smile. She rarely spoke and certainly never at the soirees she was obliged to attend. And offering a flippant opinion of love seemed to her a profanation of her wedding vows.

A messenger's abrupt entrance brought the amusement to a quick end. "Your Majesty, I have come from your brother Sujana's kingdom, where all is confusion and sorrow," the messenger kneeled before the queen. "The news is tragic. King Sujana suddenly died three days ago, and your sister-in-law threw herself into the crematory fires, declaring that this would bring her the reward of heaven."

An eruption of sorrow, both real and contrived, filled the chamber. Some of the women gasped, some fainted, and some fanned themselves. Though the queen was distraught by the news, she was proud that her sister-in-law, and by extension she herself, had proved that their love for their husbands was superior to Padmavati's juvenile infatuation for Jayadeva.

Pleased by the outpouring of support from her companions and incensed that Padmavati's show of sympathy had not been sufficiently dramatic, the queen turned to her and enquired, "Do you not think that the actions of Sujana's wife demonstrated pure love?"

"Your majesty, I humbly offer that while Sujana's wife was brave enough to face death, I do not think her act of *sati*³ was taintless. The king's messenger said that she expected to gain heaven for her sacrifice, so her actions were colored by hope of reward." Never one to dissemble, and uncomfortable with the nuances of courtly speech, Padmavati spoke as she felt.

"What audacious words!" the queen snapped.

"I do not mean them to be," Padmavati replied, eager to explain that she had meant no affront. "Yet, if your sister-in-law's motives had been truly selfless, she would not have stopped to calculate her gain but would have instantly found no use for living."

"And what would you have done?" the queen snorted, enraged that she was being upstaged in front of her own court.

"When the sun sets, its rays disappear. Likewise, I would cease to exist without my husband," Padmavati's innocent voice rang with the simplicity and finality of truth.

"Your words are insulting to my sister-in-law and show that you do not understand the meaning of love. I ask that you leave my presence this moment!" the queen commanded, pleased to have landed a crushing blow.

Now that Padmavati had been rebuked and the battle had been joined in earnest, the queen's cabal felt free to express their disdain. Whenever Padmavati passed two or more women engaged in conversation, they would whisper spiteful words just loud enough for her to hear, but separately they had not the courage to openly criticize her.

"My love, life here has become miserable for you, hasn't it?" Jayadeva had noticed a change in his wife's demeanor. "I will go to the king and ask him to permit us to return home. Your happiness is far more important to me than all the gold Lakshmana can offer us."

"You have misread me. I am fine." Padmavati had decided to conceal her unhappiness at being mistreated by the queen, thinking her predicament small in comparison with her husband's coveted position as court poet.

"I am relieved to hear that all is well, for the king has asked me to accompany him on a three-day hunting expedition. I tried to excuse myself, wanting to be with you at a difficult time, but he insisted that I go. What would you like me to do?"

"Our patron and host has invited you, so you must do as he bids."

With Jayadeva gone, it was now Padmavati's turn to be alone in the palace. She steeled herself in expectation of a fresh barrage of assaults from the queen and her clique. To her surprise and amazement, they treated her with saccharine affection.

On the third morning after her husband's departure, there came a knock on her door. The queen stood before Padmavati, ashen and tearful.

"I bring you terrible news. Your husband was mauled by a tiger and has died from the wounds!"

"It can't be true!" Padmavati's face drained of all blood.

"It is true! And here are his clothes," exclaimed two attendants as they rushed into Padmavati's room with a shredded and bloodstained shawl. The three women anxiously searched her face for a reaction, but Padmavati remained silent for a moment and then quietly closed the door.

As the queen and her companions entered the hallway, their faces darkened with malicious grins.

"So she fell for our little ploy!" said an attendant when they were out of earshot. "Your Highness, your idea of faking Jayadeva's death was masterful."

"Did you notice how she did not even shed a tear when we showed her the shawl?" observed another with venom. "She bragged that she would disappear like the sun's rays if her husband died, so it will be quite entertaining to watch her greet Jayadeva when he returns from the hunt this evening."

"I am sure she will continue to enjoy all the favors my husband bestows upon her even though she professes indifference toward them," the queen jealously concluded.

In anticipation of the return of the hunting party, the queen gathered the court that evening and eagerly waited to gloat

over her humbled enemy. She ordered one of her servants to
summon Padmavati from her room. Instead, the servant returned breathless and terrified.

"She is dead!" the servant's tone was anguished.

"What! I am in no mood for a joke."

"Your Highness, I do not lie. Padmavati's heart no longer
beats. Her body lies cold and lifeless in her room."

"No, this can't be. Call the guards! Do something!" the
queen yelped helplessly, shaken that her trick had so badly
gone awry.

Recriminations, shrill testimonies of Padmavati's virtuous
character, and disavowals of responsibility filled the court.
Soldiers ran down hallways, escorting royal physicians, who
shuffled along with their herbs and roots and mortars and
pestles. Guards ran hither and thither, trying to pacify the
queen and her wailing companions. In the midst of the
chaos, King Lakshmana returned from his hunting expedition, while Jayadeva followed behind with a second group of
hunters. Hearing shrieks and moans, the king hurried to the
queen's chambers.

After extracting a confession from his wife, Lakshmana
thundered, "What sort of a fiend did I marry? Does your
foolishness know no end? It is your ugly jealousy that has
brought this terrible disaster upon our dear ones!"

"My husband, my love, my liege, I only tried to trick
Padmavati because I imagined you were in love with her!
Now I understand that she was pure of heart. You must for-
give me!" the queen begged.

"There is no room for forgiveness. You have caused incal-
culable harm to the only friends who gave me unselfish love
and wanted nothing in return." He turned away from his
wife. When he looked at her again, she could see from his

RADHA AND KRISHNA

The love between Radha and Krishna has been celebrated in Sanskrit and Bengali love poetry for thousands of years. Esoterically, the couple is symbolic of the masculine and feminine principles of creation, the dance between Spirit and Nature, and the devotee's relationship with God.

grim countenance that he had severed his affection for her. "Wife or no wife, it is my duty as king to uphold justice. You did not believe that Padmavati had the courage to commit sati, and in testing your theory, you caused her death. Now we shall see if you and your conspirators are brave enough to walk into the flames as your sister-in-law did!"

The king ordered a great fire to be built and the guilty cast into it. But when he saw the queen cowering in terror before the roaring inferno, he said to her, "Although you deserve this punishment, I have not the heart to condemn a coward like you to death. Yet justice must be meted out, so I will give my own life in place of yours."

Hearing the king's awful pronouncement, the palace erupted in chaos. Ministers rushed to dissuade him from his rash decision. Soldiers ran about, uncertain of what to do. The queen fell sobbing at his feet. Pushing her away and waving the rest aside, Lakshmana strode to the poet's quarters to see if Jayadeva had returned and to tell him of the tragic events.

Once Lakshmana relayed what had happened, Jayadeva wailed over and over, "My Radha is gone! My Radha is gone!" The master of words, now at a loss for them, gripped a railing to steady himself, his majestic composure fleeing him.

Jayadeva turned away from the king and cried bitter tears. When Lakshmana could no longer bear the poet's grief, he walked over to him and, setting aside convention, held him in his arms.

After several hours had passed, Lakshmana said, "The bonfire beckons me, my dear Jayadeva, and it is now time for me to bid a final farewell." When he reached the doorway, he turned to speak a parting word. "There can be no atonement for the evil that has occurred in my house today. The only meager recompense I can offer is that you may take whatever you wish from the palace. Perhaps one day many years from now you will be able to forgive us."

"Lakshmana, I beg of you not to do this. What cause will be served and who will be avenged by your death?" Jayadeva continued with a strange smile, "You did not build this bonfire for those who betrayed Padmavati, nor did you build it for yourself. It is I who will cast myself into the flames to follow my wife. We have lived as one for Radha and Krishna, and we will die as one. But first, I wish to see Padmavati one last time with my eyes if they be not blinded by tears."

The two walked mournfully to Padmavati's bedroom. Once Jayadeva beheld her lifeless form, he started to sob again. Each tear that flowed was salted with an untold agony for his lost beloved.

In a plaintive wail Jayadeva began to sing, "Oh, Radha! Oh, Krishna! Hasten to my help!"

The poet's wrenching petition to Krishna echoed down the hallways. It tugged at the conspirators' hearts, and they came from the farthest corners of the palace into Padmavati's bedroom. Mesmerized by Jayadeva's song, the repentant queen and her companions joined him in earnest supplication.

Perhaps Padmavati had not died but had fallen insensate because of her grief. Perhaps she had died and the devotional demand of Jayadeva had brought her back to life. Perhaps the Lord of the Universe in his mercy interceded. Whatever the reason, Padmavati began to stir.

As the two lovers embraced, the last vestiges of their human love were purified by a divine fire, and their hearts were fused into one as they were enfolded into the great heart of God.

CHAPTER ELEVEN

Truthfulness

This above all: to thine own self be true.

—SHAKESPEARE, *HAMLET*

MIRABAI MARRIES
KRISHNA ∻

It was the winter of 1568, and the Moghul invader Babur had just sacked the city of Chittaur after eighteen unsuccessful attempts. As the fortresses's walls were breached and the last of the Rajput warriors fell, the streets ran with the blood of children, and the stench of burned flesh hung in the air as thousands of widows cast themselves into funeral pyres to preserve their honor. Unnoticed in the pandemonium, a few members of the royal family managed to escape.

One of those refugees was the elderly Princess Uda. The horrors she had witnessed and the perilous flight from Chittaur had sapped what little strength remained in her. After her arrival at a country estate far from the front, she spent many weeks in solitary grief. When she emerged from her room,

---

The great bhakti yogini Mirabai (1498–1547 C.E.) is beloved by millions in India for holding to her faith against the greatest adversities. She is considered the ideal personification of mathura bhakti—*the path in which a devotee worships God as lover.*[1]

she said little, choosing instead to pass her days thinking of Mirabai, her sister-in-law who had died over twenty years earlier, for only these remembrances gave her peace.

On a quiet afternoon, when the atrocities of Chittaur seemed a distant memory, Uda sat in the sun with her niece, Priyanka. The young woman had heard many rumors about the fall of Chittaur and was all curiosity.

"Dear Uda, is it true that our family is cursed and Chittaur fell because we mistreated Mirabai? And how is it that many of our relatives hold her responsible for our current misery, while the rest of India calls her a saint? You are the person who knew Mirabai best, so can you tell me what she was really like?" The questions tumbled from Priyanka's lips.

Uda had never shared her remembrances of her sister-in-law because they were her most painful and precious memories. But then she thought, "Perhaps the time has come to speak of Mirabai."

"Hers was a complex nature. She had an unshakeable conviction and was unyielding in her adherence to principle. Yet, she was also compassionate and caring and never had an unkind word for anyone. There was no rich or poor in her eyes. But what was most striking about her was her love for Krishna," Uda said. "I will not tell you any more about her unless you promise to keep what I say secret, for these things are not to be talked about lightly."

Priyanka nodded in agreement. Uda drew the drapes, and in the darkened chamber the world fell away as she began to speak of Mirabai's childhood.

"Mother, who is that?" asked Mirabai, pointing to a statue.

"That's Lord Krishna. He's going to be your husband," she teased.

"Why?"

"Because his love is greater than that of any man's."

"Then I want to marry Krishna and none else."

"If Mirabai had been a man, she would have been a renunciant. But she was a princess, and as you know, Rajput princesses do not renounce the world. They follow their family's wishes and are expected to fulfill the obligations of their positions. At the time of her wedding, she had not the strength to follow her heart. Mirabai thus came to be married to my brother Bhoj to forge an alliance between the House of Rathor and the House of Mewar to better fight Babur's hordes."

"What was their marriage like?" Priyanka asked. Matrimonial talk made Priyanka wonder whom her father would choose for *her* husband.

"It was a union in name only. Mirabai never showed any interest in her wifely or courtly duties. She could not bring herself to play the part of a prince's wife, nor could she tolerate the palace intrigues. In her heart, she believed that she was the bride of Krishna. Seeing him as her husband she went to great lengths to be with him, even if it meant offending every value we Rajputs hold dear. One of the most sacrilegious things Mirabai did was to pray with the peasants in the village temple."

"I would like to give you a present," Prince Bhoj said to Mirabai one day. Taking his wife's hand, he led her to a remote part of the palace grounds where there stood a marble temple. "I have built this for you so that you may worship Krishna right here."

Mirabai silently walked through the temple. Delicate stone latticework, precious gems, and a flower-decked

altar ornamented the little shrine. It was all very beautiful, but such opulence never did much to deepen her
inner communion.

"What do you think?" Bhoj eagerly asked. Though
he did not understand his wife's enigmatic heart and
was often frustrated by her indifference to his affections,
he admired her nobility and hoped to win her love.

"I am deeply touched that you would build this for
me."

"Good, then you will have no reason to sneak off to
the temple in the town or have those beggar-sadhus
come to the court!" Bhoj said.

"I do not understand why everyone else in the
palace is free to indulge their desires, yet I cannot pray
in the temple of my choice or spend my time with men
of God."

"Why can't you be like all other Rajput wives who
listen to their husbands?" Bhoj accused, furious that his
gift had failed to bring about his wishes. "I am tired of
being ridiculed as the husband whose wife worships in
the temple for commoners, ties bells on her ankles like a
temple dancer, and prances around like a mad woman!"

"By building this temple did you intend to lock me
up like a bird in a gilded cage? My soul will starve if I
cannot worship with other devotees."

"Always dramatic words from you!" Bhoj waved his
arms in exasperation. "If I were not here to protect you,
my father would have had your head for such insolence."

"At that time, I thought Mirabai was a selfish creature, cal-
lous and uncaring. King Rana, my father, had raised an army
to repel the invading forces of Babur. The shadows of war

darkened our thoughts, and the clanging of armor filled the castle halls. As our husbands, fathers, brothers, and uncles were marching off to battle, we performed *arati*[2] so they would return victorious. But Mirabai continued to go to the temple, indifferent to all that was happening around her. When King Rana discovered what she was doing, he shouted, "You wretch! How dare you abandon my son when he is preparing to give his life in battle for you! You should be setting an example for the other women of the court, but instead, you are upsetting them with your irresponsible behavior. You are undermining us at a most crucial time, and I will not tolerate it!"[3]

"I do not understand this," Priyanka exclaimed.

"As I told you, when it came to choosing between her immortal lover and her earthly husband, Mirabai's loyalty was unbending. These things are very hard to understand, especially when someone is true to their convictions even when the world stands against them."

A pained expression crossed Uda's face as she thought, "If my father had not been motivated by political calculations when arranging Bhoj's marriage . . . if my brother had not been blinded by Mirabai's beauty . . . if my family had not been so naive as to think they could break her will once she was in the palace, if . . . if . . . ! So much misery on all sides could have been avoided if Bhoj and Mirabai had never been married."

When Uda began to speak again, her eyes had a distant look, as if she were seeing before her events from the past. "My father was the greatest Rajput warrior, so I was certain that he would defeat Babur and protect my family and our kingdom. But to my horror, my brother's body was returned on a funeral bier, and my father was carried back in a palanquin like an invalid, too wounded to walk.

"I cried for Bhoj until I thought I had no tears left in me. Standing in front of his lifeless figure, I turned to see that my father had somehow pulled himself from his sickbed to mourn with us. Then Mirabai came in, the widow who never considered herself married to her husband. Everyone hated her for the pain she caused Bhoj, yet she returned our ugliness with equanimity and sympathy."

"Your presence at my son's side disgusts me," a ghastly Rana Sanga, who had lost an arm and an eye in his most recent clash with Babur, snarled at Mirabai. As if giving orders to a foot-soldier, he bellowed, "Across Rajasthan, wives of fallen soldiers are committing sati to preserve their purity. As the widow of my son, it is your duty to do the same. If not in life, prove your fidelity to him by following him in death."

"I cannot do what you ask of me."

The old warrior who had united squabbling kingdoms, who had faced Babur in battle more than a dozen times, who had earned the unswerving allegiance of his men for his bravery, stood shocked that a mere woman dared to defy him.

Rana Sanga felt like a broken old man, and Mirabai seemed to him the embodiment of strength. This feeling of weakness was new to him, and he quickly shook it off, knowing that if his allies discovered he could not command the loyalty of his own house, his fragile coalition against the invader would fall apart.

"You will commit sati." His voice was cold.

"It is not that I am afraid of death or that I even wish to live. I will give up my life for Krishna in an instant, but I will not commit sati for any other man." Mirabai was equally adamant.

"You will do as I say!" the warrior shouted.

"I will not," replied the princess.

"You better pray to your Krishna for help, for now that you no longer have my poor son to protect you, your life is in my hands."

"She refused to commit sati! What a horrible woman!" Priyanka exclaimed, even though the act of sati terrified her.

"Let me tell you the end of the story, and maybe you will feel differently," Uda replied. "My father would not tolerate Mirabai's disobedience, so he tried to kill her three times: by mixing hemlock in her drink, by putting a cobra in her chambers, and by making her sleep on a bed of nails coated with poison. Were these not despicable acts?" It anguished Uda that her father would stoop to murder to avenge his son's unhappy life. "Yet, each time she was saved by Krishna, and each time she said to my father, 'Your poisons cannot hurt me, for my Lord changes them into nectar. And even though you detest me, I bear no ill will toward you and wish you did not have to face such trying circumstances.'

"When Rana's successor, King Vikramajita,[4] ascended the throne, he imprisoned Mirabai in a palace tower, holding her responsible for our losses on the battlefield and all our other woes. I could never forget how Mirabai remained unruffled, even when she was handcuffed and led away, or how she seemed a victor despite our many defeats. Her imperturbability gnawed at me, so I secretly visited her once in the tower and soon found myself spending all my days in her presence. There I found a solace that I could not find anywhere else. I did not understand how this could be, because her body was ravaged by tribulations. But when I looked in her eyes, those luminescent and beautiful and joyous eyes, I could see that her love for Krishna had only intensified and that it had carried her through her trials. That love did not belong to this imperfect world, yet she gave it unconditionally to me and to her tormentors.

"One day, I came to Mirabai's room with a message from Vikramajita: He would release her and restore her position and wealth if she would renounce Krishna. She was staring out of the window in the direction of the village temple, and before I could speak, she said to me, 'I am dying for Krishna's love. I hear the sounds of his flute in my ears. I see his beautiful form in my dreams. Ten years as a prisoner in Chittaur is long enough. I have decided to renounce the world once and for all.'

"I said to her, 'This is unheard of! You will have to give up your title and wealth! How will you live? What will you do?'

"Mirabai smiled at me and said, 'I have Krishna, and that is all I need.' Then she removed her bangles, necklaces, and pearls, took off her silk sari, and put on a simple white robe, and with my help, she escaped forever from the palace to go wherever her heart led.

"You asked what Mirabai was like, if our family was cursed, and if Chittaur fell because we mistreated her. I can only say this: The ways of God and his saints are mysterious."[5]

CHAPTER TWELVE

Performance of Holy Rites

The reverent presentation to Me of a leaf, a flower, a fruit, or water, given with pure intention, is a devotional offering acceptable in My sight.

— THE BHAGAVAD-GITA 9:26

A MONK FOR A DAY ⌇

Every evening Keshavdas had the same harsh words for his wife, Kamala. "Your constant nagging prevents me from thinking of God in my own house! If you cannot leave me in peace, I am going to renounce my marriage vows and become a monk."

After making his nightly threat, Keshavdas would retire to his prayer room to mechanically perform his religious rites, his mind fixed on his wife's many shortcomings and wholly insensitive to the contradiction of searching for God while treating others unkindly. If Kamala wasn't making his curry too salty, she was misplacing the relics on his altar after she

---

Santoba Powar, or Santaji Pawar, probably lived in the fifteenth century C.E. in the village of Ranjana in western India, bordering present-day Karnataka and Maharashtra. A lesser-known Sikh saint, he exhorted his disciples to constantly chant "Sat Naam"—"the True Name of the Lord." He was a soldier and administrator in his premonastic life, and he took strict vows of asceticism upon becoming a monk.

had cleaned them. And if she wasn't waking him up in the morning by clanging kitchen pots, then she was putting out the wrong clothes for him to wear to the office.

It was not that Keshavdas was evil or that he did not love Kamala. Rather, he was a confused man who lived on the surface of life and believed that happiness was something that lay outside himself. A change in circumstances, he imagined, was the magical solution to all his woes.

Although Keshavdas's incessant chidings distressed Kamala, she was most pained by his accusation that she interfered with his spiritual unfoldment. When she could endure his carping no more, she sought the advice of her guru, Santoba Powar, a renowned renunciant who had given up a position of privilege for a life of austerities and meditation.

"Do not fret," Santoba said with a mischievous glint in his eye. "I promise that everything will be all right if you follow my instructions. The next time your husband threatens to leave you, tell him that you do not want to be an obstacle to his salvation and that he is free to renounce the world. Let Keshavdas know that I will accept him as a disciple."

"Are you sure?" she asked, her voice heavy with disappointment. Even though Keshavdas had caused her much unhappiness, she wanted to make her marriage a success.

"I am quite certain that Keshavdas will be a changed man if he spends even just one day with me," Santoba reassured her.

When Keshavdas returned home that evening, he launched into his usual tirade and ended with the threat of abandoning Kamala for a life of renunciation.

"I am sorry that I displease you so much." Kamala drew a breath as she gathered her courage. "I have spoken with Santoba about how unhappy you are with me, and he said that you may join him in his forest cave."

"You have told Santoba about our marital difficulties? Who else knows about this?" Keshavdas ranted, furious that his imagined reputation as a pious man and model husband might be tarnished by word of his tyrannies at home. Secretly, he was pleased that the famed Santoba had taken an interest in him, a sure sign that his spiritual worth was finally being recognized.

"I spoke only to Santoba and no one else, and I only did so because I could no longer bear to be an impediment in your search for God."

"Enough! Tomorrow I depart for the forest!" Keshavdas abruptly stood up, leaving Kamala to cry over the uneaten dinner she had cooked for him.

When dawn broke, Keshavdas smeared ash marks on his forehead with a dramatic flourish and solemnly put on prayer beads. As Kamala watched his preparations, she was stricken with the fear of being left alone, and she flung herself at Keshavdas's feet, pleading with him to stay.

"I leave you so that I may dedicate my life to a higher cause," Keshavdas said as he pushed her aside. Striding out of his house, he fantasized how he would return as a great sage many years hence to receive the homage of his ignorant neighbors and repentant wife.

Keshavdas set out for Santoba's cave, but, filled with thoughts of his own self-importance, he lost his way in the woods. After several hours of tripping over roots, falling down ravines, and wading through streams, he arrived at the ascetic's abode thirsty, hungry, and exhausted.

"Gurudev, I have come!" he announced grandly, as if Santoba had waited incarnations for this moment.

"Let us begin your discipleship immediately," Santoba said coolly. "Now that you no longer find the charms of the world enticing, you are ready to perform the renunciant's first religious rite. Take off all your clothes and jewelry. A monk has no need for such finery,"

"As you wish." Keshavdas was perplexed. He knew Santoba to be a gentle soul, yet today he was iron and ice. This must be the training he gives to his most advanced disciples, he thought, content to have found an explanation that suited his vanity.

"Now, for your second religious rite: Bathe in the stream at the foot of this hill to purify yourself of your past bad karma," Santoba said.

Keshavdas was eager to do away with lifetimes of sin just by bathing in the river. He ardently performed his ablutions and returned feeling much lighter, markedly more spiritual, and certain that he should have left his wife years ago.

"I would like to get dressed. Where are my clothes?" Keshavdas asked.

"I threw them in the river. What use are they to a renunciant?"

"Oh . . . I see." Gone were his Kolhapur sandals, gone were his Benares silks, and gone were his gold bracelets and rings! "Has Santoba no sense of the value of these things?" he angrily wondered.

"You have completed your first two penances successfully," Santoba said. "It is time for me to give you the clothes of an ascetic. Worn with the right attitude, these will bring you a satisfaction far greater than the most expensive silks."

Keshavdas pictured flowing robes. Santoba handed him a mealy rag, just large enough to protect his modesty.

"Thank you, Gurudev," Keshavdas forced himself to say.

"Now it is time for your next rite." Santoba's words weighed on Keshavdas. Giving up his clothes was hard enough, and he dreaded what was to follow. "Smear your body with this ash as a sign that you are dead to the world."

Keshavdas looked uncomfortably at the pot of ash. It reminded him of the dead. But Santoba shot him such a fiery look that he immediately obeyed.

"Now we will meditate for six hours, and afterwards I will initiate you. Do not let your mind wander or your body move, for stillness is essential if you are to be receptive to the great mantra," Santoba said.

From the comfort of his home, Keshavdas had often dreamed of sitting at the feet of saints in remote caves. But this fantasy no longer seemed appealing now that he had to actually crawl into one whose dark corners surely hid spiders and snakes. And spending six long hours in meditation seemed like an impossible undertaking when his few minutes at home were drudgery.

Keshavdas seated himself on a straw mat next to his guru and steeled himself. First, a sharp rock dug into his leg, then his back ached, and finally a fly buzzed around his face. His mind was soon similarly tormented. He had expected to be entertained by celestial visions in the company of Santoba, but instead he was stuck with his wayward thoughts.

Just when Keshavdas felt that he was going to leap up and run screaming into the woods, Santoba stirred, eyes bubbling with joy, a placid smile on his face. And Keshavdas offered a grateful prayer for having survived the six-hour ordeal.

"I trust that you feel peaceful and nourished?" Santoba inquired.

"Well . . . yes," Keshavdas lied.

"I am glad to hear that because today our food comes from God."

"What do you mean, Guruji?" Keshavdas apprehensively asked. He had not eaten since his half-finished meal the previous night, and after spending the early morning walking and all afternoon meditating, he was famished.

"Today we fast," Santoba stated. "But if your body needs to eat, I would be happy to give you my begging bowl."

"I am an important man! How can I go into town and beg for food? And in this loincloth! I cannot do it." Dejected by his dilemma, he sat down chin in hand. Then he had an inspiration. "Can you go for me?"

"You must know that one cannot be a renunciant by proxy. If you are truly giving up the world, then you must forget that you once were a man of means and power," Santoba replied sternly. "As for your food, go to town and beg for it, or find the strength to fast for one day."

What little self-control Keshavdas had, he quickly mustered to squelch his ire. As a government official, he had commanded the respect of his subordinates, as the master of his house, he had lorded over his wife. Yet, here he was being chastised as if he were a bumbling novitiate.

"As a disciple, you cannot pick and choose which rules you would like to follow," Santoba said in answer to Keshavdas's unspoken thoughts. "Go collect some firewood so that we can stay warm this evening and keep away the animals. The walk will do you good."

Keshavdas picked up every stick, resentful that his teacher considered kindling more valuable than his life. As dusk approached and the forest came alive with screeches and howls, he hurried back to the cave, apprehensively looking over his shoulder every time he heard an ominous sound. While he stared into the darkness, fearful that bloodthirsty predators caused the rustling of leaves, his unperturbed guru chanted verses from some ancient scripture. Finally, Santoba signaled that it was time for bed.

"Where do we sleep?" Keshavdas looked around the barren cave.

"These rocks are our pillows and the ground our bed. We forest ascetics sleep hugging Mother Earth. Soon enough you will become used to our ways. Now go to sleep."

Santoba immediately began to snore. Keshavdas lay awake, thinking of his soft bed at home with its mosquito nets and his wife lying by his side. As he drained the bitter dregs from his cup of self-pity, he found a new appreciation for Kamala. She was, in truth, a loving and selfless woman who cared for him, yet he had returned her kindness with ingratitude and contempt. How he wanted to put an end to this ill-conceived adventure!

"Master, wake up, wake up! I can't take this anymore! I am not an ascetic. I will never be an ascetic. I do not have the fortitude to perform these holy rites. I want to go home. I miss my wife," Keshavdas whimpered.

"I do not keep my disciples here by force," Santoba replied between yawns.

"How can I return to town looking like this?" Keshavdas pointed to his ash-smeared body. He jumped up, terrified that Kamala might not take him back, that his neighbors might have heard of his foolishness, and that his office had found a replacement for him.

"You have been here for just one day, and look at all the problems you have caused me!" Santoba said in mock aggravation.

"You don't understand!"

"Please calm down, and I will help you. But before I do, I wish to talk to you."

Keshavdas grimaced, anticipating another humiliation.

"It is admirable that you desire God, but you have erroneously believed that spiritual progress is only possible through the renunciation of familial ties. You have forgotten that the circumstances that you attract are the ones that are most beneficial for your spiritual growth. And when you perform your holy rites, it is your thoughts that should be your only concern, not some outward show of piety. Practicing rituals while the mind remains fixated on others' imperfections is of little value."

"All my years of pujas have been in vain!" Keshavdas moaned dispiritedly.

"The Gita says that no good effort is ever lost. Your habit of daily worship will serve as a foundation for spiritual growth if you are serious about deepening your inner life. You will know you have made real progress when you can endure the trials of daily living with equanimity."

"It seems that it is better for me to be a good husband and practice a little religion than to be an ascetic who dreams about curries and a soft bed," Keshavdas felt as if he had lived many years since the morning.

"Your understanding shows that you are ready for initiation." In Santoba's soft voice, Keshavdas once again recognized the kind-hearted guru that his wife revered. The sage whispered a mantra in his ear and continued, "As for helping you further, I will go to your wife tomorrow and tell her that if an ash-smeared ascetic should show up at her door in the middle of the night, she should not be afraid. It is her repentant husband who has returned, and he is a wiser man for spending one day as a monk."

CHAPTER THIRTEEN

Study of the Scriptures

Thy Self-realization will blossom forth from thy soulful study.

—PARAMAHANSA YOGANANDA

A LEAP OF FAITH ॐ

"Ramananda! My favorite armchair philosopher! So once again you are up with the birds, poring over your musty scriptures," Brahma Dutt teased his neighbor from the balcony across the narrow lane. Yawning lazily, he queried, "What are you reading this morning? Krishna dancing atop a serpent's head? Rama hunting a demon disguised as a golden deer?"

Ramananda amusedly looked up from his palm leaf manuscripts. "Laugh if you will, but these scrolls help me make sense of a universe that can seem strange and baffling."[1]

"Let no one ask a man's caste or with whom he eats. If a man is devoted to Hari, he becomes Hari's own," thus declared Ramananda (1400–1480 C.E.), a pioneer of the Bhakti movement in North India.

Born in Allahabad, Ramananda developed his own interpretations of self-surrender and devotion to God, which came to be called "Sri Sampradaya," a tradition distinct from all other Vedantic sects. Without regard to caste, creed, and gender, he accepted Hindus, Muslims, and untouchables[2] as his disciples, and for this he earned the derision of the orthodox. Kabir, Ravidas (said to be the guru of Mirabai), Dhanna, and other great Sufi and Bhakti saints were reputed to be among his students.

"How can such an intelligent man like you waste time with these silly myths?" Brahma Dutt delighted in ridiculing Ramananda for a childlike faith he wished he possessed. The loss of a loved one a few years ago had turned him against his Maker. Since that time, life seemed cruel, and as a consequence, trust and openness became strangers to his heart. Now he used skepticism as a shield to cover the wound.

"Great wisdom is hidden in what you call fairy tales. Just think of the Sundara Kanda, which I am about to study today." Ramananda's face glowed as he imagined the saga of Hanuman, Lord Rama's greatest devotee.[3]

"Ah, ha! The profound tale of the monkey-god that jumped across the ocean! I am sure your simian warrior's antics will keep you engrossed for days on end."

"A literal reading of this story is foolish. Valmiki chose to make his hero, Hanuman, a monkey to show that even the most restless of creatures can master the mind through attunement with the guru," explained Ramananda.

"What an illuminating lecture. I know I do not have your intellect, but Hanuman jumping a hundred miles to cross an ocean somewhat stretches credulity. Don't you agree?"

Ramananda's reply was a patient smile as he returned to his scrolls. Thus far he had read how Hanuman and his search party had traveled south looking for King Rama's wife, Sita. For many days and nights, they had marched through dark forests and climbed impassable mountains searching for the missing queen.

"We are low on rations and exhausted from our quest, and now an infinite ocean spreads out before us," a warrior despondently said to Hanuman.

"Our quest has come to an end. It is time for us to return home," said another.

"It is better for us to take our lives than fail Lord Rama," Hanuman answered. The others agreed and began piling logs for a pyre.

Engrossed in the story, Ramananda became Hanuman. He could feel the heat from the fire as it blazed on the beach, and his chest tighten with grief for having failed his guru.

"I have seen Sita," said Jatayu, an old vulture who overheard the soldiers' lamentations. "The evil king Ravana took her across the ocean in a flying chariot to the city of Lanka a hundred miles away."

"A hundred miles! That is uncrossable," a warrior dejectedly exclaimed.

Jambavan, the leader of the brigade, replied, "As death is our fate today, we can leap and fall into the sea and drown, or jump into flames and be consumed by fire. It is far better to die trying than to die in defeat."

Valiant Angada, a young commander, spoke, "If one of us can reach Lanka and find the whereabouts of Sita, our mission will have been successful."

Ramananda thought, "If we could discover some useful information in Lanka that might help Rama in a final assault, it would be well worth giving our lives." In a fevered trance he continued reading.

"I can jump fifty miles!" cried a young soldier.

"I can jump seventy-five, but that still would not help our cause," moaned Angada.

"I am old now, and with the greatest effort, I think I can jump ninety miles," said Jambavan.

All the warriors turned to Hanuman, who sat quietly

by the water's edge. To succeed in an insurmountable
task such as this required one with stupendous faith.

A fierce ocean wind blowing in his face, Ramananda
stood up and paced the shoreline, pondering his dilemma.
"Can I put my guru's needs before my life? Do I have the
strength to cross the ocean?"

A thud on Brahma Dutt's roof brought him running up
the stairs. "What is going on here?" He saw Ramananda
sprawled on his rooftop, blood trickling from his head, the
manuscript held tightly in his hand, and a look of rapture on
his face.

"I have crossed to Lanka!" Ramananda's voice seemed
otherworldly.

"Are you all right?" Brahma Dutt exclaimed in amazement, seeing that his neighbor had jumped from rooftop to
rooftop and had narrowly missed plunging to his death. As he
looked at Ramananda, the bliss in the devotee's eyes stole
into his heart.

Brahma Dutt thought, "What is it about this man that
makes him so radiant? Whatever he has, I want. Perhaps it is
time to make peace with him. And perhaps it is time to make
peace with my Maker." "You are a most unusual scholar,
Ramananda. If you permit, from tomorrow may I join you
in the study of the scriptures?"[4]

HANUMAN

Embodying the qualities of loyalty, intelligence, nobility, humility, and courage, Hanuman is portrayed as having such tremendous physical strength that he is able to lift mountains and uproot trees in the service of a noble cause.

CHAPTER FOURTEEN

Subjugation of the Senses[1]

The more one yields to desire, the more insatiable it will become.

—THE MAHABHARATA

VEMANA MENDS HIS WAYS

"Vemana, though I am your sister-in-law, you know that I have loved you as a mother. That is why I must say the truth even if it is hurtful. You have become addicted to gold, wine, and women." Subbamma's candor was fired by several years of praying for her prodigal brother-in-law to reform.

"It is not true that I love only gold, wine, and women. I care equally for all pleasures," Vemana chuckled. Seeing Subbamma wince, he quickly added, "You are the most precious thing in the world to me. So you see, I do love something more than my vices."

"Then for the sake of whatever feelings you have for me, please mend your ways before you become so depraved that you no longer recognize yourself."

"I wish I could heed your advice, but I am who I am.

Vemana (seventeenth to eighteenth century C.E.) was born in Andhra Pradesh in South India. A prolific poet who traveled widely, Vemana wrote over 3,000 simple quatrains with deep wisdom, which are still taught to schoolchildren today.

This is my nature, and it is fruitless to fight it. Would you ask the sun to stop shining or the wind to stop blowing?" Vemana was pleased with his irrefutable logic. "And now, my beloved sister-in-law, I must go, for I have an important engagement."

Subbamma's heart darkened, for she knew what kind of pressing appointments Vemana had. His days were spent on the outskirts of town in caves with alchemists trying to turn lead into gold, while his evenings were passed in a drunken daze in houses of ill repute. Though Subbamma tried to look beyond Vemana's indiscretions to see the sensitive boy who had been orphaned as a child, her sympathy of late was in short supply. If her husband, Anuvemareddi, a minister who served in the king's court, were to learn that his younger brother had stolen money from the royal treasury to finance his escapades, the family would be ruined.

And so Subbamma began to weep because she had failed to be the mother that the boy had needed. Vemana, meanwhile, had already forgotten the conversation, for he was consumed with the newest object of his affection: the prostitute Kamakshi.

"Was there ever a woman like Kamakshi?" Vemana savored this thought with a smile as he made his way to the brothel. It gave him unending delight to fantasize about her bewitching banter, the shapely lines of her legs, and her hennaed hands feeding him betel leaves. She was all grace and elegance, he liked to imagine, though in truth he knew she was a coarse woman.

"I have a special favor to ask of you, my darling," Kamakshi cooed after they had been together. She frequently asked Vemana for money and presents knowing that he came from an affluent family, and he always obliged.

"Anything for you. Ask the world and it shall be yours!" Vemana heroically exclaimed.

"Your sister-in-law, Subbamma, has the most exquisite jewels. I would like to wear them for a day." Before Vemana could object, she continued. "Just think how beautiful I will look wearing them. I will be your pleasure princess! I know that a powerful man like you can do anything."

"I cannot ask Subbamma for her jewelry! They were her wedding presents!" Vemana loved to ply Kamakshi with gifts, but this request was too outrageous for him to even consider.

"Then I cannot see you again."

After several minutes of threats from her side and supplications from his, Vemana conceded. Once they had professed their mutual, undying love, he left on his errand, utterly at a loss as to how he could convince Subbamma to loan him her jewelry.

As he neared his home, he remembered all the times his sister-in-law had indulged him, and he calculated that Subbamma's generous nature would not allow her to refuse his request. "I will tell Subbamma the truth," he thought. "I am in love with Kamakshi, and she desires to wear your bangles and rings for one day." As soon as Vemana began to talk, though, his rehearsed speech sounded hollow, and shame nearly strangled his tongue. Subbamma listened incredulously, for such a request could only mean that he had become Kamakshi's puppet and that she was using him to snatch the family fortune.

"If I lend them to you for one day, will you promise that you will never speak to me again about your mistresses' fancies?" Subbamma hoped that if Vemana could no longer provide Kamakshi with gifts, she would quickly lose interest in him.

"Yes, yes, whatever you want! I promise."

"Don't speak so lightly! Lending my jewelry to a prostitute is unspeakable, but I will still do it. Here! Take them! Remember, this is the last time I will help you."

Puffed like a peacock, Vemana brought his loot to Kamakshi and triumphantly presented it to her. She greedily grabbed the glittering ornaments from his hands, put them on, and preened in front of a mirror. At the end of the day, with a histrionic show of tears and tearing of pillows, she grudgingly let him take them back to Subbamma.

Hardly a week passed before Kamakshi made an even bolder demand: that Vemana fetch Subbamma's wedding necklace. Once again the drama of threats, concessions, and reconciliation was played out. Kamakshi shouted. Vemana equivocated and, finally, yielded.

"My beloved sister-in-law, I have come to you for another favor," Vemana said. Since he had flippantly promised not to ask her for more gifts, he assumed that Subbamma would know this and oblige him one last time. After all, had she not been tolerant of his foibles thus far?

"You ask for my wedding necklace?" Subbamma gasped in horror after Vemana had finished speaking. "Do you not realize that it is the symbol of my marriage to your brother? Without it, I will be considered a widow or, worse, a fallen woman."

"Kamakshi demands that I bring it to her if I am to ever see her again," Vemana said, deaf to his sister-in-law's distress.

"I cannot agree to this. You are breaking my heart."

When Vemana arrived at the brothel, he showered Kamakshi with caresses and flattered her with unctuous words. Scarcely concealing a weary impatience, she tolerated his affections for a little while and then pushed him away to ask if he had brought the necklace.

"My sister-in-law refuses to part with it," Vemana complained.

"You have come to me without Subbamma's necklace?" she roared and slapped him. "You say that you love me, but you fail to fulfill my slightest wishes. What kind of a love is that?"

"I will buy you a more expensive one," Vemana offered, hoping to placate her.

"I don't want a nicer one. I want hers!" Kamakshi's face became mottled with rage. "Are you too dumb to understand? I need her necklace if I am to walk among decent people without them snickering at me. Get out of my presence, and don't return until you have fetched it for me!"

"But . . . but . . . Kamakshi!"

"Get out! Get out!"

Mad with despair, Vemana stumbled out, his mind inflamed with anger, self-loathing, and a thousand other blistering emotions. He broke into a run, not knowing where he was headed, and he stopped only when he found himself in a gloomy forest far from town.

"Those lips, those eyes! Never mine again. How can she be so unreasonable! All this fighting over a stupid piece of jewelry! And Kamakshi says she loves me? Why can't Subbamma part with it? Her and her self-righteous lectures. Yet, she has always helped me and would give it to me if she could. Oh, I wish I could die and be through with all this!" His chaotic thoughts tumbled in such quick succession that they left him panting.

Morning found Vemana in a crying heap at Subbamma's feet. She saw in him a man on the verge of insanity. His clothes were soiled with sweat and dirt, his face tight and grim, his eyes bloodshot and wild.

"I know what your necklace means to you, but I cannot

live without Kamakshi!" Vemana sobbed after he relayed to her the events of the evening.

After a moment of thoughtful quiet, Subbamma said, "Oh, Vemana, you must be tortured to ask me for such a thing! So I will give my necklace—not so that you may win the affections of this horrible woman but because I fear that if I don't, you will resort to some madness."

A pathetic smile lit Vemana's tear-stained face.

"Meet me in three days at the ruins of the old Siva temple near the cremation grounds on the outskirts of the city. There you can take it from me."

The intervening hours were sweet for Vemana. Kamakshi slavishly attended to his every whim and fancy, and his agony in the forest quickly seemed nothing more than a disturbing dream. On the third day at dusk, he bid Kamakshi farewell, promising to return in a few hours with the necklace.

Humming a tune, Vemana made his way to the ruined Siva temple. When he saw its crumbling pillars, the overgrown weeds feeding on its walls, and the vandalized stone statues, the song died on his lips. Walking in the gathering gloom on sacred grounds where the dead were once honored was so disturbing that he was jerked out of his intoxicated stupor. The smell of Kamakshi's perfume lingering on his silk shirt caused him to shudder and remember Subbamma's warning that depravity would pervert him beyond recognition.

"Subbamma, Subbamma, where are you?" Vemana called nervously, the sinister meeting place filling him with dread.

Following her instructions, he entered the temple. He spied candlelight at the end of a corridor and quickened his pace. In the flickering light, he saw a figure swathed in a long robe. It was Subbamma, as pure as ever, but her countenance was ghastly.

"Vemana, my son, I am here as promised," Subbamma's voice was distant. "You have asked for my necklace. You know what it means to me. If you still want it, you will have to take it yourself." As she finished speaking, she cast off the robe she was wearing and stood naked before him.

"Oh, my God! Subbamma, what are you doing?" Vemana shielded his eyes with his hands as his knees crumpled under him.

"Take my necklace and you will have stripped me of everything. But take it if you must!" Her words were as a knife twisting into his heart.

"What a sewer of iniquity I have fallen into!" He had believed he could keep company with the degenerate and remain untouched. Now he knew that he was one of them. "For lust of a prostitute, I have defiled the sanctity of your marriage. I have betrayed my brother and humiliated you. I am an ungrateful wretch who has returned your motherly love with deception and selfishness. There can be no redemption for a sinner like me!"

Subbamma moved to console him.

"Mother, my lust has turned me into a beast! Please do not come near me, for I am all corruption and am afraid to contaminate your purity. I must kill my desires before they will kill me."

Vemana rose up abruptly and fled. Finding a small cave, he sequestered himself in it and mercilessly bore into his soul until the cause of all desire stood revealed. When he returned to Subbamma many years later to ask for forgiveness, she looked at him and began to cry tears of joy, for she could see that there was a new light in his eyes and that temptation had a hold on him no longer.[2]

CHAPTER FIFTEEN

Nonslanderousness

Judge not, that ye be not judged. For with what judgement
ye judge, ye shall be judged: and with what measure ye mete,
it shall be measured to you again.

—MATTHEW 7:1, THE BIBLE

EIGHT TOPICS OF
CONVERSATION

After the monks of the Jetavana Monastery had finished their
dinner, they gathered in the common room to pass the evening
in conversation.

"I am appalled at King Ajatasatru's cruelty. Have you heard of
his latest brutalities?" a monk asked the other men at his table.
This ignited a heated conversation about the despot's misdeeds.

At a table on the other side of the room, another monk
spoke. "A new fragrance has arrived in the market. I hear that
all the women have fallen in love with it."

---

*The Tipitika (Pali, "three baskets") is a collection of essential Pali language texts
that form the doctrinal foundation of Theravada Buddhism, a form of Buddhism
practiced in Sri Lanka and some other parts of Asia. One of the "three baskets" is
called Sutta Pitaka, which is a collection of over 10,000 suttas or discourses deliv-
ered by the Buddha and his close disciples. The fourth division of the Sutta Pitaka
is the Anguttara Nikaya (the "Further-Factored Discourses"), and it is here, in
Nikaya X:69, that this story is originally recorded.*

"Always something to keep the people distracted from the goal!" replied a novitiate with contempt.

At another table, one monk asked his brothers for advice. "Mahendra Varma, the finance minister, came to the monastery the other day, bragging how he has reformed himself by following the teachings of the Buddha. But I have heard from a reliable source that he is the greatest of sinners. I cannot stand such hypocrisy. Do you not think it is my duty to tell him of his errant ways the next time he comes visiting?"

So went the brothers' banter, one moment an observation that sparked an argument, the next an anecdote that elicited contentious opinions. A hush fell over the room as the Buddha entered the dining hall after having spent the day meditating in the forest.

"What have you all been talking about so animatedly?" the Enlightened One asked. After they had answered his question, the Buddha replied, "Such topics of conversation do not befit men who have renounced the world. Gossiping like this will do you great harm."

The monks understood the Buddha's words to mean that every judgmental or base thought held within it the seed of evil. These would eventually sprout and degrade the mind of the speaker. A mind so disturbed and sullied would be unable to behold the true nature of things, making the goal unattainable.

"If you are to talk, O Monks, these are the proper topics of conversation: having few wants, contentment, solitude, virtue, concentration, discernment, the knowledge of the teachings that lead to liberation, and liberation. Speak of these noble things, and you will outshine the sun and the moon and the stars."

CHAPTER SIXTEEN

Modesty

Take the lowest place, and you shall reach the highest.

—MILAREPA, *TREASURY OF SPIRITUAL WISDOM*

THE FLAWED POT ⌇

"Namdev, how dare you insult the Lord by singing your silly little songs while I am conducting holy Vedic rites?" snapped a Hindu priest, envious that his congregation ignored his grandiloquent chanting in favor of a tailor's spontaneous songs of devotion. The bilious priest went on. "If you are unable to keep a respectful silence in the sanctum sanctorum, you are free to croak at the edge of the temple precincts."

Namdev respectfully heeded the priest's order and started to sing at the temple gate. The priest, however, soon found

---

Jnaneshwar (1275—1296 C.E.) is one of the founders of the Varkari tradition—the path of traveling pilgrims who sang songs of love for God. Considered by many to be the greatest saint of Maharashtra, he inspired a religious revival. Jnaneshwar is also remembered for his philosophical treatise, Bhavartha Deepika ("Light of the Inner Meaning"), also called Jnaneshwari, which brought the highest of Vedic thought within reach of all.

Jnaneshwar's circle of friends—Namdev the tailor, Gora Kumbhar the potter, Narhari the goldsmith, Chokamela and his wife the outcasts, Sawata the gardener, and Janabai the maidservant—all went on to become great devotees of Lord Vithoba of Pandharpur.

this arrangement to be even less satisfactory, for one by one the devotees stopped attending his services, choosing Namdev's divine melodies at the entrance instead. Then a strange thing happened: All the accolades started to seduce Namdev, and with each passing day he increasingly sang for his audience instead of God, forgetting that the Maker of the Universe, and not he, was the fount of all inspiration.

One evening, Namdev and the sage Jnaneshwar found themselves at the home of a mutual friend, the potter Gora Kumbhar. The three men, along with the potter's family and a few other guests, enjoyed savory curries, sweets, and pleasant conversation.

"Namdev, I love listening to your songs!" Gora Kumbhar said as Namdev struggled to suppress a satisfied smile.

As the diners lingered over their dessert, Jnaneshwar cleared his throat. Everyone fell silent, understanding that the esteemed teacher wished to speak.

"Have you ever thought that we are like pots?" Jnaneshwar began curiously. "Some of us are well-made vessels and as a result are of great worth to the One we wish to serve. Others decorate a shelf and have no practical use. And some pots, though they look sound, have hidden cracks, making them of no value at all."

"My friend Gora, every day you make pots of different sizes, colors, and designs. After you throw the clay and bake the pot, do you not tap them with a stick to find out which are fit for sale and which have flaws invisible to the eye?"

"This I do," replied Gora, bemused by the question.

"As you can see, there are many pots in this room," Jnaneshwar continued as he pointed to the guests. "Can you please do me a favor by picking up your stick and tapping all present on the head to see if they are sound?"

An odd request indeed, but Gora Kumbhar agreed, having a great respect for the sage. He reached for a stick and started going around the room tapping each guest lightly on the head.

"This is fit for sale," Gora proclaimed, and everyone chuckled. "This one, too. Here is another well-made pot."

When Gora reached Namdev, he angrily knocked the stick away. "How dare you treat me as if I were a pot! Have you forgotten that I am a devotee of Lord Vithoba!"

Gora cringed at Namdev's sharp response, but he picked up the stick and continued.

"What have you found?" Jnaneshwar asked when he had finished.

"All the pots here are sound except for one," Gora replied and then pointed to Namdev. "This one here has not been properly baked."

The laughter of the guests pricked Namdev, and the more he blushed, the more humor they found in his embarrassment. Humiliated at being the object of their amusement, he rushed out of the house, ran to the temple, and threw himself in front of the altar, bitterly complaining to the Lord about the insult he had received from enemies disguised as friends.

For the first time in many weeks, Namdev chanted for God and not for self. Then he understood and prayed, "My beloved Lord, you have given us abundantly of your creative inspiration. Our talents are only thy gifts, temporarily ours but ever returning back to thee, neither increased nor diminished by what we do."[1]

After many hours of prayerful contemplation, the Lord finally spoke to Namdev as a friend. "When Gora Kumbhar went to tap you, you refused because you lacked the modesty to be one among equals. This happened because you have become enamored of the praise of my devotees. Would you have their admiration and be forgetful of me, just like the priest in my temple, or would you rather remain obscure to all but be ever with me? Love me and not the flattery of others, and I will give you all that your heart seeks."[2]

CHAPTER SEVENTEEN

Lack of Restlessness

To see a World in a Grain of Sand
And a Heaven in a Wild Flower,
Hold Infinity in the palm of your hand
And Eternity in an hour.

—WILLIAM BLAKE, *AUGURIES OF INNOCENCE*

OF LEDGER BOOKS AND LIBERATION

"Listen, and I will first tell you a truth about men and then a secret of the spiritual life," spoke the teacher, Janardan, to his young student, Eknath.

Since Eknath had become a disciple, he had never asked for instruction, and his teacher had never offered it. Being in the company of an enlightened sage was enough for Eknath, and he was content to cook his guru's meals, clean his home,

---

Eknath (1533–1599 C.E.) belonged to an illustrious and saintly family from Maharashtra. His grandfather, Bhanudas, was a pious and brave man who restored the famous statue of Lord Vithoba in Pandharpur after it had been forcibly removed by Rama Raja, a king of a neighboring province. Its return sparked a religious revival in Maharashtra. Eknath's father, Suryanarayan, was a sage who earned acclaim during his own lifetime. Given the status of his forefathers, the boy Eknath wanted to prove himself worthy of his noble lineage.

and wash his clothes. So to hear his master, who was always
pressed by countless responsibilities, make such an unusual
offer caused the young student to sit upright and listen attentively.

"The rishis have said that man's mind is like a drunken
monkey stung by a scorpion, jumping from one thing to another. This restless desire is the cause of man's misery. You
have seen a proof of this in those who have come to me for
instruction but could not withstand my discipline even for a
month. I ask you to consider this: If a seeker is too impatient
to do a simple household chore, how can he be entrusted
with something as sacred as a mantra?"

Eknath remembered the dozens of young men who had
arrived, eager to start their discipleship. After a few days of
cutting potatoes and cauliflowers, their enthusiasm would
wane, and they would start to grumble how they were wast-
ing their time in menial work when they should have been
receiving sacred teachings. To them, liberation lay in any
place other than their present surroundings. These disgrun-
tled disciples would eventually fail to show up for their duties one morning and would never be seen again.

"Now I will tell you a secret of the spiritual life: The con-
centrated mind is a key to success in the search for God, for
if one cannot focus the mind to accomplish small things, it is
utterly incapable of apprehending the infinite."

Eknath had seen Janardan meditate without distraction for
many hours. He also remembered stories about his own
grandfather, the sage Bhanudas. It was said of him that he
would sit unmoving in singleminded prayer to the Lord.
Eknath had often wondered if he would ever have the same
strength of purpose.

Janardan spoke again, "I have carefully watched over you

since the time you ran away from home and came to me seeking truth. You have diligently performed your ashram duties and are now ready to assume greater responsibilities here. Henceforth, I entrust you with keeping track of the king's accounts. Every evening before you go to sleep, I would like you to reconcile them."

Tallying the hundreds of entries in the royal ledgers was a laborious and painstaking chore. As soon as Eknath finished his evening meal, he commenced work, spending hours at the task. Day after day he faithfully performed his new duty.

One evening when he completed his calculations, he found that there was a discrepancy of one rupee. So he checked his math, only to arrive at the same figure. Again and again Eknath added up the accounts, but each time he came up short of one rupee. The hours passed, and the rows of numbers turned blurry as he checked the piles of invoices against the entries. Although he grew weary, he was determined to please Janardan, and he wanted to solve the riddle hidden in the ledger books as his little offering of perfection to Krishna.[1]

"I found it! I found it!" Eknath cried as he finally discovered his mistake.

"What is happening here?" It was Janardan who spoke. He had left the office the night before and had just returned to start a new day, only to find Eknath still sitting at the desk, the table-lamp covered with soot and its wick burned out. "Have you been up all night?"

"Yes, sir. You asked me to reconcile the ledgers and I have done so." Looking up with a victorious smile, Eknath was surprised to see the sunlight streaming through the curtains. He had been adding and readding the numbers for twelve hours. Then he explained the saga of the missing rupee.

"Your singlemindedness pleases me. I am proud of you. You have the makings of a good disciple." Janardan patted his shoulder.

"Thank you, sir, but I only reconciled account books." Eknath was mystified by his teacher's uncharacteristic praise.

"God is in ledger books, too. A man's character is revealed in the smallest thing he does." Janardan beamed. "Your attentiveness and persistence show that you are now ready for initiation. If you meditate with the same intensity with which you kept your mind on this ledger, you will quickly reach God."

SARASWATI

The goddess of learning and wisdom, Saraswati's name is composed of two Sanskrit words—*sara* "essence" and *swa* "self"—which can be translated as "knowledge of one's essential self." She holds a *veena* (a stringed instrument) in her hands to show that attunement with the true Self produces the music of harmony.

Because the swan is reputed to be able to drink only milk from a mixture of milk and water, it stands for perfect discrimination and serves as a reminder for the spiritual aspirant to discriminate between that which is beneficial from that which is harmful.

CHAPTER EIGHTEEN

Perseverance in Acquiring Wisdom and in Practicing Yoga

Perseverance is the whole magic of spiritual success.

—PARAMAHANSA YOGANANDA,
MAN'S ETERNAL QUEST

MILAREPA BUILDS
A TOWER

"I have climbed the high mountain passes of Tibet for many days in search of Lama Marpa Lotsawa. Do you know where I can find him?" spoke the young man, Milarepa, to a tall monk with penetrating eyes.

Considered one of Tibet's great saints, Milarepa's (1040–1143 C.E.) life story is still widely retold. A man renowned for his intensity of spiritual striving, his teachings live on in the Kagyu school of Tibetan Buddhism. In fact, the head lamas of this school still trace their lineage back to the great yogi. Milarepa is also known for the "Hundred Thousand Songs of Milarepa," which capture his deep devotion and faith and recount the events in his life and those of his disciples.

Though Milarepa was born and lived in Tibet, we have included him in the book for a number of reasons. He is a seminal figure in the yogic tradition (he called himself a yogi) and is still widely revered as a saint by many esteemed Hindu gurus and millions of Indians. Also, the spiritual lineage to which Milarepa belonged can be directly traced to India—Marpa, Milarepa's guru went there to receive the sacred teachings, Marpa's guru was Indian, and many other elements in this narrative harken to the country's spiritual traditions.[1]

"Finish plowing my land, and I will tell you where you may find him in the village of Drowo Lung," said the monk, taking measure of the traveler whose dust-covered clothes bore silent testimony to a long and difficult trek.

Milarepa zealously took to the task, thrilled that he was nearing the end of his long search for a guru. As soon as he finished, he ran to the small house where the monk lived and respectfully waited for him to finish his evening meal.

"Do you not know who I am? Prostrate before Marpa!" the monk roared as he wiped his sleeve over his mustache. "What do you want from me?"

"I wish to be your disciple and humbly ask permission to make a full confession of my many sins."

"You may speak if you keep it brief," the lama curtly replied.

Milarepa quickly gathered his thoughts. Anxious that he not further irritate the esteemed teacher, he spoke with haste. "When I was young, my father died. The relatives who were the custodians of my inheritance disregarded his wishes and kept the money for themselves. This reduced my mother and me to poverty. After suffering for many years, my mother grew mad from despair and craved vengeance. She sent me to a master of black magic to learn his art, and as soon as I was proficient, she ordered me to take revenge on those who had betrayed us."

Milarepa stopped for a moment, tortured by the memories of past misdeeds he was about to recount.

"I went to the house where all my relatives were gathered and cast a spell that caused it to collapse. Thirty-three people died." His voice breaking under the strain of guilt, he continued, "Since that day several years ago, I have been in agony. Now I want to be free of my past and dedicate my life to the search for liberation. I will do anything to achieve it, and that is why I have come to you. Will you accept me as your disciple?"

Milarepa anxiously searched Marpa's face for a reaction, but the lama stared out of the window disinterestedly and then picked at a thread on his robe. A few moments passed in silence.

When the lama next spoke, his voice was hard. "I fear that you may not be fit for the spiritual life because of your evil past." Seeing the desperation in Milarepa's face, he softened ever so slightly. "So that you do not think my heart is made of stone, I offer you one of two choices. I will give you food and clothing until you find another teacher, or I will instruct you, but you must provide for your own food and clothing."

"I choose you as my guru!" Milarepa blurted.

"My instruction is not like learning magic tricks from a charlatan. Your training here will be quite different." Then Marpa ominously added, "Before you so hastily take me as your guru, hear this: Once you are my disciple you must unconditionally submit to my will. If you ever resist, I will cut you to pieces."

"I will never resist." Milarepa ignored Marpa's provocations, for being accepted as a disciple was enough for him.

"It is time to begin your training. Come with me," Marpa barked. Walking outside, he led Milarepa to a field near the monastery. A crown of majestic rock and ice, the Himalayas, ringed Drowo Lung and its terraced foothills. Marpa spoke again, "The secret teaching I know is so powerful that if you are sincere and devoted, you will attain enlightenment in this life. But before I give it to you, I demand that you complete one task."

"Whatever you ask of me, I will do," Milarepa pledged,

confident that he could accomplish anything Marpa asked of him with just a little more effort than it took to learn black magic.

"See the rocks lying in this field? Build for me a round tower on the eastern ridge of the nearest hill with them. You may come back to me when it is half completed."

Milarepa stifled a gasp. The stones in the field were of considerable size, and the eastern ridge was a steep climb of several hundred feet. It would be a back-breaking task. Sensing his reluctance, Marpa looked at his disciple disapprovingly.

"I will come to you when it is half done," Milarepa replied eagerly to show his willingness.

Grunting with exertion as he lifted the first rock, Milarepa began to struggle up the slope. The weight of the granite was so great that he had to change his grasp every few feet, yet balancing it on his shoulders or putting it on his head made it no easier to carry. Panting with exhaustion, arms burning from fatigue, he finally reached the eastern ridge.

Milarepa dropped the stone, sat down on it, and wistfully looked at the monastery. Monks were moving across the courtyard to gather for prayer. Sitting on this lonely ledge, he wished he were part of that sacred brotherhood, but this was not to be until he completed the tower. Spurred by the hope of wearing the saffron robe some day soon, he raced down the hill with renewed vigor to bring up the second stone.

Hour after hour, day after day, week after week, Milarepa carried the heavy stones up the peak. Each trip was its own unique trial in endurance and left some mark upon his body—a bruise, a scrape, or a missing fingernail. When night fell and he could no longer find his way, he stumbled into Drowo Lung to beg for food. He voraciously ate what the villagers were kind enough to offer and then collapsed into a deep slumber, forcing himself to wake up with the morning's first light to begin another day of labor.

As the days of spring lengthened into summer, the mound of rocks on the hill began to rise and take the shape of a tower. When it was half complete, he sought out Marpa in the joyous anticipation of receiving the secret teaching.

"I do not like the tower where it is, Great Magician," Marpa said, his words dashing Milarepa's hopes. "Tear it down and bring the stones back to the field."

Milarepa looked perplexedly at Marpa, but then he remembered his vow of unconditional obedience. Perhaps he had misheard what the lama had wanted, he rationalized. And so, he began carrying the stones down the mountainside.

Once his disciple had brought all the stones back to the field, Marpa said, "I promised that I would give you the sacred teaching as soon as you completed the assigned task. I would like you to build for me a semi-circular tower on the western ridge. Come for me when it is half-built."

Milarepa listened carefully to his guru's commands so as not to misinterpret them and began carrying stones up the even steeper western slope. The harder the sun beat down on him, the harder he worked. When the first scent of autumn filled the air, Milarepa sought out the lama to show him what he had accomplished.

"Oh, no! I must have been drunk when we last spoke. Tear it down!" Marpa said as soon as he saw the tower.

"Tear down the tower?" Milarepa's voice cracked in disbelief.

"Now that I am free from the influence of the grape, I can see that this is not at all what I had wanted." Marpa seemed utterly indifferent to the consequences of his fickleness. "Bring the stones back down from the mountain, and come to me when you are done."

For a moment, Milarepa's thoughts were all darkness: Marpa was a moody madman. Yet, men of the highest discrimination and intellect from all corners of Asia sought him out for spiritual guidance. This meant the lama could not be insane. So up the western ridge he trudged and down he came with the stones.

On the first evening of autumn that carried the chill of winter, Marpa summoned Milarepa and said, "I have pondered long about this, and I want you to build me a triangular tower on the north ridge of the hill. Please do this, and once you finish I promise to give you the secret teaching."

"I will gladly build you a tower. But before I begin again, are you sure this is what you want?"

"How dare you ask such a question? Do you think I am drunk? Or mad?" Turning away in disgust, Marpa continued to shout to himself, "My teacher, the great master Naropa, was attacked by wild dogs, wolves, snakes, and all sorts of terrifying monsters as a test to see if he was worthy enough to even meet his teacher. And now this one, with lifetimes of bad karma, comes and complains to me because I asked him to carry a few stones!"

"Please, let me finish the tower!" Milarepa pleaded.

"As you wish," Marpa pleasantly replied and walked away. "Remember, the north side!" he smilingly added.

As the first snows of winter covered the ground, Milarepa began to build a tower on the steepest of all the ridges. Sharp winds knifed through the valley, the days grew short and gray, and still he inched up the icy trail. Toiling in the frigid air caused his skin to split, leaving running sores on his shoulders and hands. Whereas the work had been difficult during spring, summer, and fall, in the darkness of winter it was excruciating.

One dreary day after a few weeks had passed, Marpa

demanded of Milarepa, "Why are you building a triangular tower?"

"Sir, what do you mean? You asked me to build it for you!" Milarepa replied with tears of frustration.

"I made no such request! Do you have a witness?"

"No!"

"Maybe you are building a sorcerer's tower to work your dark magic on me!" Marpa accused. "That tower is filled with evil spirits! Destroy it immediately!"

"And then what would you have me do?"

"Start a new tower with stones untainted by your spells," Marpa answered as though his command was perfectly reasonable.

Milarepa quivered in rebellion at the lama's nonsensical whims, but what was he to do? To leave Drowo Lung would mean forsaking his search for liberation and returning to the world as an unredeemed murderer. Better to suffer Marpa's capricious commands so long as hope for salvation remained. So he labored through knee-deep snow, tore down the tower, carried the rocks back to the field, and brought up new ones. Though his hands and back bled, and he shivered from being exposed to the bitter winds, he plodded on, desperate to finish before his resolve faltered.

One day late in March, as the first blossoms stirred from their winter's sleep, Marpa came to Milarepa.

"The tower on the north ridge is quite beautiful, but I now realize that it is far too steep a climb for an old man like me. I want you to build me a square tower nine stories high in this field. Just think how delightful it will be for me to enjoy views of the countryside from the top. And once it's finished, I will give you the secret teaching!" Marpa said, ignoring his dumbstruck disciple's horrified expression.

"Sir, this is the fourth tower I will build for you. Each time you gave a different reason to tear down the previous one. Before I start the next one, I humbly ask that your wife, Dakmema, be a witness to our agreement."

"Of course, of course," Marpa mischievously nodded and sent for her.

As Milarepa began constructing a square tower in the field, several of the lama's disciples took pity on him and helped him move a large cornerstone. The work went quickly, and soon Milarepa had built two stories.

"Mighty Sorcerer! How did you move that giant rock that is the cornerstone?" Marpa enquired one day. Hearing that it was done with the assistance of three other monks, the lama said, "You deceived me by enlisting the help of someone else. Remove that stone, and put it back by yourself."

"But, sir, I will have to tear down the tower to do that!"

"Remove the stone, or find another teacher: You may decide."

"Do you know what the people of Drowo Lung are saying?" Milarepa could no longer contain his frustration. "Marpa has gone mad and has ordered an idiot of a disciple to build and demolish tower after tower to no purpose."

"If you have no faith in me, then it is best that you leave."

And so Milarepa tore down the tower and began to build it again. When he had completed the seventh story, Dakmema came to him.

"A disciple from Tsangrong has arrived today with offerings for the master in the hopes of receiving initiation tonight. Take this turquoise, and give it to the lama as your gift, and perhaps he will be disposed to initiate you as well," Dakmema said kindly.

When Milarepa entered the monastery, he saw the lama warmly embracing the disciple.

"My heart is filled with joy that you have made it to Drowo

Lung!" Marpa showed keen interest in the new arrival and plied him with questions about his travels. "It must have been an arduous journey crossing those high mountain passes. You should rest, my son, for this evening I will initiate you into the secret teaching."

"Oh, Master, it is true what they say about your kindness: It is unsurpassed!" The student exclaimed.

After ordering a young monk to take good care of the guest, Marpa turned to Milarepa and said, "Ah, Great Magician, what do you want?"

Hearing his name spoken shook Milarepa loose from the web of thoughts in which he had become entangled. It was stupefying to see the lama so warmly receive a new disciple when he had been vainly laboring for months with curses and humiliations as payment.

"May I also receive initiation tonight?" Milarepa ventured as he offered the turquoise Dakmema had given him.

"How dare you ask for such a thing when you have failed to complete the one task I assigned you!" Marpa stood up and lunged at Milarepa. He grabbed him by the collar and kicked him in the behind. "Get out of the monastery, and don't return until that tower is built!"

Crushed by an avalanche of aggrieved questioning, Milarepa stumbled out. Had he not begged for his own food? Had he not built the tower four times already? Had he not nearly killed himself carrying stones for the lama?

Milarepa wandered until he reached a stream. He splashed water on his face and neck to douse his wrath. Watching the clouds pass in front of the moon, he wished that he could be carried with them to some far-off land on the other side of the mountains where his troubles could not follow. When his mind finally became lucid, he thought, "I am in darkness on account of my sins. I am the author of my own misery."[2]

Reasoning that if he had written a black fate for himself he could write a better one, he resolved that he would continue to carry the stones up the north slope. And if he could not walk, he would crawl, and if he could not crawl, he would drag himself until his work satisfied Marpa.

The next morning, Marpa came to Milarepa as he was mixing mortar.

"Evil Wizard, I wish you to stop work on the tower. It is high enough." Hope leaped within the disciple's heart until Marpa spoke again. "I want you to build a shrine room on the first floor with twelve columns around the base of the tower. Once you finish, I will initiate you into the secret teaching."

Surmising that his guru's comparatively modest request signaled the end of his long labors, Milarepa took to his work with a renewed enthusiasm. Though his spirit was willing, his back was an inflamed mass of sores that prevented him from lifting stones. Seeing Milarepa suffer, Dakmema ministered to him, putting balm on the lesions. Distraught by her adopted son's agonies, she requested an audience with Marpa.

"Look at him, my husband. Not even a pack mule has sores like this. He is not fit for work anymore!" Dakmema pulled away Milarepa's shirt.

Marpa sternly replied, "Yes, these wounds are bad, but they are not nearly as painful as what my guru had to endure before he was accepted by his teacher, nor are they as severe as the tests that I had to undergo."

"You have never treated any other disciple like this. Can you not show him a little mercy?" Dakmema interceded.

"All right. All right. Let us make an ointment for him. As soon as he is feeling better, he can begin work again." Looking at Milarepa with that mischievous grin, he said, "Finish the shrine room, and I promise that I will initiate you into the secret teaching."

Milarepa thought bitterly, "The lama lies, this body is broken, and I can no longer drag myself. This tower will never be finished, for Marpa will surely want to add another room, a wall, a garden, a walkway, and on and on. I am done."

Lying awake that night he remembered his resolution to work until he pleased his guru. Now it seemed foolish to him, and even more ridiculous was the year of titanic effort he spent moving stones. In despair he decided to leave Drowo Lung to find another teacher. On the eve of his departure, he sought Dakmema to bid farewell.

"Milarepa, you are so close to finishing your work. How can you stop now?" Dakmema asked. "Come, let us go to the master. I will plead with him on your behalf!"

"I no longer believe that he will initiate me, so I must go." An unspeakable sadness filled his heart as he resigned himself to wander through the desert of mortal life without spiritual consolation.

"Perhaps there is still a way you can receive initiation," Dakmema spoke after a long silence. Milarepa's heart quickened. "I will write a letter in my husband's hand asking Ngokpa, his disciple in Kyungding, to initiate you."

Forged note in hand, Milarepa left for Ngokpa's monastery. He presented the letter and was initiated. Ecstatic that he had the technique, he locked himself up in a remote cave and, forgoing food and sleep, meditated ceaselessly. But he did not feel even a hint of peace despite his colossal striving. And he knew this was because he had deceived his guru.

After many weeks had passed, Ngokpa came to Milarepa's cave.

"I have received word that Lama Marpa himself has finished building the tower in Drowo Lung. He is going to dedicate it, and he has invited the "evil-doer" and me to the inauguration. Do you know to whom he refers?" Ngokpa asked.

"I am the evildoer," Milarepa replied, pained by the broken vow of discipleship. "I will go with you to Marpa."

How different it felt to come to Drowo Lung, not as a sincere seeker filled with the hope of redemption but as a fallen disciple who had lied to his guru. When he saw the remnants of the towers he had built on the mountainside, he lambasted himself for not persevering unto death. He thought, "My sufferings on the mountain were nothing next to the anguish I now feel for having betrayed Marpa!" As he entered the hall, he was too ashamed to look up from his feet, and he wished he could vanish into the shadows.

"When you first came, you had told me that you had murdered thirty-three people. What new sins do you have to confess, wicked sorcerer?" Marpa asked by way of greeting.

"You had said that my evil past made me unfit for the spiritual life, and I have proven your words to be true." Despondency choked Milarepa's voice. In halting words, he narrated to the lama how he and Dakmema had colluded to trick Ngokpa.

In a show of anger, Marpa shouted, "I had not wanted to accept you as a disciple, but you pestered me into doing so. Then I tried to give you special training, but you complained at every turn. Now you tell me that you have dragged my wife and senior disciple into your net of deception. You know that loyalty is the highest law in the spiritual life, and yet you deliberately betrayed me!"

"I am dying of shame and have come to offer an apology."

"What use are your apologies? Get out of my presence," Marpa ordered.

Milarepa ran out of the hall, up the hill to the steep north-

THE WHEEL

Representation of wheel from the famous sun-temple at
Konarak, Orissa.

Built by King Narshimha Dev-I of Ganga dynasty in 1250
C.E., the Sun temple of Konarak is a single monolithic sculp-
ture in the shape of a chariot. It is said that 12,000 sculptors
worked for twelve years to erect it. The wheel as a symbol is
important in both Buddhism and Hinduism.

ern ridge, and to the edge of a precipice. Seeing the tower that Marpa had completed in his stead far below threw his mind into a suicidal whirl. Jumping would be a painless way to end his life.

"Milarepa . . . don't," cried Ngokpa as he chased him.

"What reason have I to live? I am so damned that even my apology was not accepted. There is no refuge for me in this life."

"You cannot kill yourself. It is the greatest of all sins." Ngopka tried to reason as Milarepa moved closer to the cliff's edge.

A young monk came panting up the slope. "Milarepa . . . Ngokpa . . . the master wishes to see you!"

These words snapped the spell, and Milarepa, used to obeying Marpa's commands, climbed down from the ledge. Waiting at the monastery gate was the lama, who lovingly embraced his disciple.

"It is time for me to explain my bewildering behavior," Marpa said as the monks of the monastery gathered to hear the answer to the mystery of the past twelve months.

"Many years ago, I had a vision in which I saw the one who was to be my greatest disciple, a young man with a stalwart heart but much bad karma. I impatiently waited for him to come to me. When he did arrive, I gave him the most drastic training, knowing that this would be his quickest route to liberation. Milarepa, my son, you are the one I saw in that vision.

"You had to pass through nine ordeals to expiate your sins. That is why I ordered you to build the towers and tear them down over and over again. That is why I seemingly treated you so capriciously and cruelly. But you must know, my son, as you struggled to carry each stone up the mountain, I suffered with you. And when you could no longer endure, I carried your karmic debt by finishing the last tower for you."

"Who has ever heard of such an unselfish love?" Milarepa wept. "To think I dreaded the shadow of the hand that was in truth outstretched in blessing!"

"Because of your undaunted perseverance and devotion to truth, and your steadfastness and determination, you will achieve liberation in this life and will attract many good and worthy disciples who will share your zeal and wisdom. They will willingly follow you on the pathless path to nirvana."

CHAPTER NINETEEN

Absence of Greed

How far that little candle throws his beams!
So shines a good deed in a naughty world.

—SHAKESPEARE, *THE MERCHANT OF VENICE*

THE GOVERNOR'S
LAST DAY ⌒

On a scorching midsummer day under a blast furnace of a
sky, the ministers from the province of Mangalavatam gathered together on a shaded verandah to honor the retiring
Governor Damaji for a life given in service.

Vito Pant, next in line for the governorship, said, "I put
this crown on your head to show that you are the king of
our hearts."

"Before I turn over the responsibilities of my office to such
a capable man as you, I have a final question," Damaji said to
Vito. The assembled guests, annoyed by a morning of tedious
tributes and irritated by the heat, feigned a respectful silence.
"Today I read a report that the drought affecting many states

---

*Damaji Pandit, or Damaji Pant, was a devotee of Vithoba, who probably lived in
the sixteenth century C.E. His life story is recorded in the Bhaktavijaya, a treatise
composed by Mahipati in 1762. One of the lesser-known saints of Maharashtra,
Damaji devoted the latter part of his life following the Varkari tradition of wandering pilgrims established by Jnaneshwar.*

of India has worsened. In the waning hours of my tenure, can you reassure me that all is well in our district?"

"I have received no petitions for aid, and the royal granaries are full," answered Vito Pant, who also oversaw the food stores. "Governor, you have been an inspiring example of enlightened leadership to all of us, but now it is time for you to rest. Go in peace. The Lord is smiling upon Mangalavatam!"

"Then let us put aside the concerns of the state and enjoy this buffet before us!" the governor said, even though he had little appetite for such elaborately prepared dishes and kept a simple diet.

Within a few minutes, the governor was all but forgotten as the discussion moved from days gone to the days that lay ahead. The passing of the reins of power to Vito Pant was a topic far more interesting to the guests than encomiums about the governor's moral rectitude.

Damaji watched the affair feeling more like a spectator than the guest of honor. The last few years had been like this too. Since the king had appointed Vito Pant as the next governor, Damaji had perceived a subtle change in those around him. Slowly but undeniably, the loyalty of his ministers had shifted from him to his successor. He fought against this at first and then resigned himself once he understood that these subtle betrayals, though disheartening and even a bit humiliating were inevitable to those who had fallen from power. The years of demanding service had also sapped his vitality, and though he loathed to acknowledge it, he felt old.

Seeing Damaji tremble from fatigue and the heat, the captain of the guards brought over a chair. He returned when he saw that Damaji had been sitting alone for quite some time.

"Governor, I want to tell you that you have been an inspiration to me for thirty years." The captain of the guards spoke. "I never once saw you use your position for personal gain. Even though vast sums of wealth were at your disposal, you lived as simply as an ascetic. Whether it was day or night, you always received those who requested an audience and listened to their woes with sympathy and patience. Mangalavatam was blessed to have a man like you at the helm of our government."

"Your words are too kind. All I did was follow the Dharma."

"No, sir, you did far more than that. In fact, I worry about you. I fear that you have been so generous that you neglected to set aside anything for your old age."

"It does not require much to go on pilgrimage," Damaji smiled.[1]

A crash in nearby bushes interrupted their conversation. Out stumbled a man who wore the sacred thread of a Brahmin. Emaciated from starvation, he teetered on bony legs. In his lifeless eyes, hollow cheeks, and jutting ribs, Damaji saw the face of famine. And he feared that the Brahmin's plight portended a catastrophe.

"Kind sirs, have mercy! I have been walking for four days without food or rest." The Brahmin's eyes rolled up in his head, and he fell backward. Damaji and his ministers rushed to his side.

"Take him into the house, and put cool water on his lips to revive him!" Damaji ordered his attendants. "Once he has recovered, dress him in clean clothes and bring him to me."

"Governor, your service is ended. I will take care of this emergency." Vito Pant reassuringly patted Damaji's hand. Turning to the captain of the guards he barked, "Send orders for your regiments to immediately double the guard at the granaries. Have them start patrolling the bazaars and mercantile districts. Arrest anyone suspected of looting, and enact a curfew in the town beginning tonight. We do not want a combustible situation to explode."

"A combustible situation?" Damaji asked uncomprehendingly.

"There is word of unrest in the other provinces, and we want to prevent something untoward from happening here. I kept this from you because I did not want to upset you."

"Yes, yes. You did not want to upset me. Of course," Damaji mechanically replied. He thought, "Have I grown so feeble that my ministers do not want to tell me what is happening in Mangalvatam?" Watching Vito Pant move with such decisiveness and vigor, and seeing the other ministers so solicitously look to him for guidance, Damaji felt like a useless old man.

Once the party had resumed, Damaji made a large plate of food and quietly disappeared into the governor's mansion to seek out the Brahmin. The man lay in a small room, sipping water. "I brought this for you," Damaji placed the food before the weakened man.

"I cannot bear to look at this food, knowing that my wife and children are nearly dead from hunger. My conscience will not allow it. Please, take this away from me." Tears rolled down the Brahmin's cheeks.

"You are an extraordinary man to put the love of your family before your own life. But you are not well and you need to eat. Take some food, tell me what troubles you, and I promise that I will help you," the governor insisted.

As the man began to speak, Damaji beheld a vision of vultures flying across a barren landscape to alight on human carcasses, their curved beaks picking and tearing at the flesh. And he was mortified.

"I am a schoolteacher from Pandharpur, who has been reduced to misery. This famine has robbed me of everything. Rice and wheat have become so expensive that the merchants seem like moneylenders. I had to sell all our possessions to buy food for my family, and after I spent our last few rupees, we survived on roots and berries. With all the townspeople in the same dire condition, there was soon nothing left to forage. We were so desperate that my wife and I left our son and daughter at home and set out determined to find food or die trying."

"After wandering for two days, we met a kind traveler who gave us two fistfuls of rice. We gratefully accepted his gift, but it was not enough for even one of us. My wife, who was too weak to go any farther, sacrificed her portion for me so that I might eat and have the strength to walk to your residence and petition you. Your generosity is renowned, and we thought you might help our family."

In Damaji's long tenure, he had witnessed the parade of human misery in all of its hideous variety, but he had never heard so distressing a story. "I will have my attendants fill four bullock carts with food and escort you back to your home. You can now eat in peace."

Damaji strode to his study and slammed the door in a rage. He put both hands on his desk to hold himself up, weighed down by the burden of the years. "How I have failed my people and my king! So much misery! So much suffering! All because I have been asleep. The good that I have done these many years has come to naught."

As Damaji berated himself, the Brahmin hurriedly ate and set off with two soldiers to Pandharpur. After traveling a short distance, the earth seemed to open up and spit out a stream of wraithlike men and women. They trailed the Brahmin from a distance, their desperate eyes fixed on the carts. As they silently closed in, he nervously looked to the guards for assurance, but the guards seemed equally terrified. Sensing that the crowd was about to lunge, the Brahmin held out his arms and shouted, "No! No! This is food for my starving children! Have pity."

In a tidal wave of desperation, the mob knocked him to the ground, overwhelmed the guards, and plundered the wagons. The mayhem lasted all of a minute until the carts were laid bare, and then a deathly silence descended as the villagers vanished like mirages. Pulling themselves up, the soldiers stood shivering, while the Brahmin remained on the ground, bloodied and beaten.

"Brahmin! Brahmin!" One of the soldiers shook him by the shoulder. "Come to your senses!"

"The scriptures say that this world is an ocean of suffering, and I have seen this with my own eyes. Now that I have a full stomach, I can go home and watch my children die."

"Let us go back to the governor. He is understanding and will surely give you more food," one of the guards said consolingly as he lifted the Brahmin to his feet.

The three men started back to the governor's mansion, but they had traveled only a short while when the mob reappeared, now larger than before. "They are following us because they think we know where food can be found," said a soldier. "We must hurry so that Governor Damaji can call out the guards!"

Taking the whip to the oxen, they rushed back to Mangalavatam. Interrupting each other, they agitatedly told Damaji how a mob had attacked them and looted the carts and how they were lucky to have escaped with their lives. Before they could finish their tale, hundreds gathered outside, their shrill cries for food reverberating throughout the governor's mansion.

Walking to the window, Damaji saw the guards struggling to control the surging crowd. Infants howling, mothers pleading, young men fighting, the old pushed underfoot— the people of his province, once so peaceful and prosperous, had been reduced to savagery.

"You assured me this morning that all was well in Mangalavatam, so why are my people wailing?" Damaji searched his ministers' faces, and each one turned away guiltily.

"I am as surprised as you, but now is not the time to conduct an investigation," Vito Pant said, and he then addressed the captain of the guards. "Order your men to disperse this crowd before there is a riot."

The captain of the guards hesitated, waiting for Damaji to confirm the command.

"Why do you want to use force against our own people when their need is legitimate and great?" Damaji asked Vito Pant. "Is this what you learned from me?"

"Old Man, I don't have time for your moralizing! Will you stop asking questions and go off on your pilgrimage?" Vito Pant shouted. Pointing his finger at the captain of the guards, he said, "Obey my order! Crush this riot!"

The captain of the guards looked at his friend one last time and then moved to leave. And Damaji knew that this was the defining moment of his life. He thought, "If I do nothing, the courtyard will run with the blood of thousands of innocents. And if I act, that will anger my ministers, and they will seek revenge when I am no longer in power."

Pulling himself up like an aged warrior for a final battle, Damaji said, "Belay the order. I am still the governor until sunset. These people need food, not a beating. Open the king's granaries and distribute the grain until they have had their fill!"

"Make this your last decree, and I will see to it that you hang for it!" Vito Pant hissed.

"Yes, yes, such a deed deserves death," the other ministers chimed in a chorus.

"Why would you not open the granaries? Oh, my Lord! Now I understand!" And then all the threads of the day came together, and Damaji knew that a viper had been by his side, spitting the poison of flattering words in his ear. "You are all conspirators in a vile plot to starve the people for profit. You knew of this famine, and instead of distributing the king's grain to relieve the sufferings of the poor, you have colluded with the merchants to sell food at usurious prices. It is just like what the starving Brahmin said."

Vito Pant was discomfited for a moment, but he quickly regained his composure. In his fall, though, Damaji saw that his confidence was bluster, his power, cruelty.

"You are a poor beggar with not a rupee saved for your old age. I offer you half the gains in this business if this secret dies with you," Vito Pant tempted. "Of course, if you choose otherwise, as the new governor I will see that you meet an unfortunate end on one of your pilgrimages."

"He who lives by the Dharma is protected by the Dharma,"[2] Damaji said with equanimity. "Captain, we have much harm to undo. Open the granaries! As for you, my ministers, I will deal with you once this crisis is over."

Word of Damaji's benevolent decree quickly spread across the province. The hungry came—first as a trickle, then as a river, and finally as a flood. Day after day, in ones and twos, as families and as entire villages, they made their way to the granaries. Standing in lines that stretched for miles, they patiently waited and took what they needed. Praise for Damaji's kindness rang on every street corner and city square until the king's soldiers appeared with orders for his arrest. They bound him and brought him to the king's court and made him stand trial.

"Your ministers have accused you of selling my grain for your personal profit. They say you did this because you were leaving office without a rupee of your own. What do you say in your defense?" asked the king.

"Your Highness, these charges are false." Damaji then told the story of the starving Brahmin and how Vito Pant had plotted to choke off the food supplies so he could enrich himself.

"What do you have to say to this?" the king asked Vito.

"My liege, it is preposterous for Damaji to claim that he is the only good man in Mangalavatam and that everyone else is corrupt. In fact, his twelve ministers will attest to the truth of my accusation."

All eyes anxiously turned toward Damaji to see how he could possibly extricate himself from the noose tightening around his neck, for Vito Pant was a darling of the court whose eloquence had charmed everyone.

"Your Highness, the riches I seek are not of this world. My only desire these past few years has been to go on pilgrimage, and for that one needs little money. And if greed was my aim, then I could have amassed a fortune during my stewardship." Damaji's earnestness was beyond reproof. "I have fulfilled my duty to you by distributing your wealth to your subjects in their time of need. If you still doubt my veracity, I have a simple solution. Instead of asking my twelve ministers, ask any twelve people of Mangalavatam if I opened the granaries because I craved gold or because their need was dire. I am content to place my fate in their reply."

The king pondered for a moment and then spoke,

"Damaji, for three decades you have faithfully served me, so I found these charges hard to believe. Still, in the interest of justice, I had to hear out your accusers. I will ask twelve people from Mangalavatam why you opened the granaries. If they respond as you say they will, I pity Vito Pant. Now unchain this man!

"Men of courage and character like you are rarely found. You have shown that a man of selflessness can do great good in the world. Your actions were noble and holy." Then the king stood up and declared, "Let everyone here understand my wishes. All the royal granaries across India are to be opened until no one suffers from hunger."

CHAPTER TWENTY

Gentleness

When a man has true knowledge, he feels everything is filled
with consciousness.

—RAMAKRISHNA, *TREASURY OF
SPIRITUAL WISDOM*

NAMDEV FEEDS A DOG

"There goes crazy Namdev," said one shopkeeper to another.
"Look at him, singing and dancing like a drunken man. And
he is so absurdly thin. I hear that he never eats."

"Leave him be. He may be a fool, but he is a fool for the
Lord."

"If this is what it means to have God, then I'd rather stay
the way I am."

So went the daily debate among the people of Pandharpur
over Namdev, one who was so intoxicated with the love of
God that he would forget the needs of his body.

When Namdev beheld a bed of flowers, he saw God hid-

---

*Namdev (1270–1350? C.E.) earned his place in the canon of India's saints for his
intense devotion and his composition of simple songs to the Lord, called
Abhangas. Married and a father of five, he retreated from the world for long pe-
riods of time to meditate, especially later in life. Both Hindus and Sikhs consider
Namdev a saint. In fact, eighty of his hymns have been included in the Guru
Granth Sahib. Though he was from western India, he was so beloved that a tem-
ple was built in his honor in the northern and predominantly Sikh province of
Punjab.*

den in the blossoms. When he looked at an ant, it was the Creator of the Universe who had taken that humble form. And when he gazed upon mountains, there he perceived the Lord in his majesty. But his favorite way to worship God was as Lord Vithoba, the deity of the village.[1]

Absorbed in love for Vithoba, Namdev's days sweetly sped by. He would wake up, say a prayer, and make his way to the river at dawn to wash away the impurities of body and mind. Then, he would go to the temple to join the early morning worshipers and awake the Lord from his slumber with songs of praise. Namdev and the devotees reverently watched the priests bathe the statue in the temple with holy water, dress it in new clothes, deck it with flowers, and offer it food. When the temple reopened in the evening, Namdev and his fellow villagers gathered in the courtyard to hear bhagavatars tell stories of saints. The day closed with Namdev putting Vithoba to sleep with lullabies.

And so, dawn turned to dusk and dusk to dawn several times before Namdev, engrossed in his devotions, noticed that he had not eaten. A kindly housewife, seeing his wan appearance, said with sisterly concern, "Namdev, you have become a skeleton without food. Here, take these few chapatis and some ghee so you won't go hungry."

Namdev gratefully accepted the food, returned home to his thatched hut, put the chapatis and ghee on a small mud stove in the corner, and sat down to pray to Vithoba for taking such good care of him.

The patter of clawed feet on the dirt floor of his hut interrupted Namdev's meditation. A mangy dog, more bones than flesh, held the chapatis in its mouth. Seeing Namdev stir, the dog bolted from the house. Namdev grabbed the ghee and ran after it.

LORD VITHOBA

Representation of Lord Vithoba, also known as Panduranga or Vitthala, from the temple at Pandharpur (sixth century C.E.), one of the revered pilgrimage sites in Maharashtra.

"There goes crazy Namdev. Now he's chasing a dog!" said the shopkeeper.

"Why does he have that cross expression on his face? And is that ghee in his hands?" said another, amused by the spectacle of the village fool chasing a ragged mutt.

As fast as the dog ran, Namdev somehow ran faster. Finally, he cornered the animal in an alley.

"Why are you running away from me?" Namdev questioned the frightened dog, as if speaking to a close friend who had hurt him. "You cannot eat chapatis without ghee. They will be tasteless and dry and stick in your throat. Here, let me put some ghee on them for you."

Forgetting his own hunger, Namdev gently fed the dog as if he were Lord Vithoba.

CHAPTER TWENTY-ONE

Straightforwardness

Self-realized sages behold with an equal eye a learned and humble Brahmin, a cow, an elephant, a dog, and an outcaste.

—PARAMAHANSA YOGANANDA, *GOD TALKS
WITH ARJUNA: THE BHAGAVAD-GITA*

RAMANUJA DISOBEYS HIS GURU

From the moment Ramanuja had come into this world, he had been consumed with a desperate yearning to find a solution to the cause of all suffering and share it with all. When scholarship, discipline, and theological debate failed to satisfy him, he sought out Nambi, an esteemed teacher who was known to be the keeper of an esoteric technique of meditation that was said to be the panacea for all ills.

"Ramanuja, I purposely denied you spiritual instruction

Born around 1000 C.E., in the village of Perumbudur, Ramanuja was raised by a pious, well-to-do family of the Brahmin caste. As a youth, Ramanuja decided to forsake worldly life and become a renunciant. Author of commentaries on the Brahma Sutras, Vedanta Sutras, and the Bhagavad-Gita, Ramanuja also traveled widely, expounding the worship of Vishnu as a means for salvation. His life and teachings inspired many including Ramananda, and Jayadeva, the saint-poet of Bengal.

to measure your character," Nambi said after his disciple had walked seventeen times from his home in faraway Srirangam to the hermitage in Madurai. "Because you have won my trust and have shown that you are willing to endure hardship for a greater good, I will initiate you into the most powerful mantra in our tradition tomorrow at dawn. It has been passed down in secret from guru to disciple for hundreds of generations. With reverential repetition, it will bring you closer to God."

The monks present stood amazed that Nambi was willing to initiate him after a discipleship of only a few years, for the teacher was known to be an orthodox disciplinarian who did not easily part with the mantra.

That night seemed an eternity to Ramanuja, and the hours could scarcely pass fast enough. He lay awake in anticipation of winning his own liberation and helping others win theirs. When the sun's first rays crept above the horizon, he rushed to meet Nambi at the appointed place.

As he made his way, he watched the people of Madurai waking to a new day. Merchants were leading their bullock carts into the market, and Ramanuja fretted with them over their profits and losses. Farmers were going to their fields to begin another hard day's work of tilling and sowing, and he worried with them that this year's harvest would be poor. An old man was sweeping the street, and in his stooped frame he felt the weight of a long life of sweat and toil and humiliations. Ramanuja sorrowed to think that every one of them plodded through the years as the living dead, hypnotized by the belief that unhappiness was their natural state.[1]

In kinship for his brothers and sisters, Ramanuja found his mind reaching out and embracing all those around him and expanding into the far reaches of space. He felt the colossal whirling of galaxies and heard every atom and every living thing the cry in agony from being separated from their Creator. And he was horrified that the Lord's children fitfully slept under a miasmic blanket of maya in a night of unhallowed darkness.[2]

"What can I do now that I have seen the truth?" Ramanuja thought as he staggered to the temple. When he saw Nambi standing solemnly at the entrance, he tried to bury his distress. His guru led him into a small chamber hidden behind the altar. Looking around to make sure they were alone, Nambi beckoned his disciple to come nearer, placed a shawl over both their heads, and began to whisper.

"Ramanuja, you are the one I have chosen to be the guardian of the mantra and my spiritual heir. When I leave this world, I will place in your charge my ashrams and gold, and I will make you responsible for training my monks and ministering to my householder disciples. Though you will have much wealth, the most precious of all your possessions will be this mantra. Anyone who repeats it will be freed from the threefold sufferings of bodily, mental, and spiritual woes."

"But before I give you this great spiritual key, you must make a promise: that you will safeguard it from superficial seekers and will reveal it only to those worthy disciples you deem to be your successors," Nambi exhorted gravely, for a mantra of this power was only for those of the Brahmin caste.[3] As a final warning he added, "If you share it with those who are not worthy, you will suffer eternal damnation."

"I promise I will bestow it only on those I deem worthy," Ramanuja replied.

"It gives me peace that I can entrust you with this," Nambi whispered in his ear. "Om Namo Narayanaya."[4]

Ramanuja's soul took flight as he began to utter the holy

GOPURAM

Sacred spires found in South Indian temple architecture.
Colorful and towering, these magnificent gateways
enclose the *sanctum sanctorum*. Signaling the holy destination
was in sight, the *gopurams* often sent traveling pilgrims into
raptures.

words again and again. Then he abruptly stood up, bowed to his guru, and resolutely left the dark chamber.

"Where are you going?" Nambi inquired as he followed, perplexed by his disciple's strange behavior. "I have just given you initiation, and now you should sit in silence and practice."

Deaf to his guru's pleas, Ramanuja ran to the towering gate at the entrance of the temple grounds. As though his feet had wings, he flew to the top.

"My dear people of Madurai, your brother Ramanuja beckons you. Come to the temple gate!" he cried aloud, turning north, south, east, and west, his voice booming down the streets. "Come! All who are sick in body shall be healed. Come! All who are weighed down by worries shall find solace. Come! All with a zeal for salvation shall find it."

The merchants in the markets, the farmers in the fields, the housewives in their homes, and even the downtrodden stopped and listened. They had never heard such a glorious promise, and they streamed out of the bazaars and the alleys and flocked to the temple gate. All the while, Nambi remained rooted in place, appalled by the blasphemy that was about to occur.

"The great mantra that I have just received from my master will take you to celestial realms," Ramanuja addressed the multitudes. With a voice so loud that it seemed as if it would break the sky, he chanted, "Om Namo Narayanaya, Om Namo Narayanaya, Om Namo Narayanaya."

The chant alighted upon the lips of everyone, and a holy chorus rose up to the heavens. Peace descended on all as God came to each in the manner in which they prayed, and new hope blossomed in arid hearts. Filled with bliss, Ramanuja descended from the temple gate. Nambi waited angrily below.

"Why did you do this?" the Guru asked, furious that his favorite disciple had betrayed him.

"Gurudev, I did not break my promise. I gave the sacred mantra to those who were worthy. For are not all souls worthy?" Ramanuja bowed his head awaiting judgment. "If you do not feel as I do, I am happy to suffer eternal damnation knowing that I have helped my brothers and sisters find freedom in God."[5]

CHAPTER TWENTY-TWO

Self-Discipline

Give me chastity and continence, but not just now.

—ST. AUGUSTINE, *CONFESSIONS*

TULSIDAS RUNS OFF TO HIS WIFE

"Tulsidas, it is customary for a new bride to go to her parents' house during the first festival after the wedding, yet several have passed, and you have not let me return home. I miss my family. Will you let me visit them?" Ratnavali implored her husband, who listened impassively.

Although Ratnavali's request was natural for a bride recently separated from her family, it was fraught with the unspoken difficulties of an unhappy marriage.

Life with Tulsidas was far from what she had hoped, for he was a man of contradictions. He would spend hours with scholars, discussing the scriptures and the transitoriness of

---

Tulsidas, one of Hinduism's great saint-poets (1532–1623 C.E.) was orphaned at an early age and grew up in a Hanuman temple, living on offerings made by passing pilgrims. A scholar, impressed by his intelligence and devotion, raised him as his own. Tulsidas went on to compose the Ramcharitmanas, *a poem of unsurpassed beauty that has been called the greatest work of Hindi literature. His compositions are still dear to devotees of Rama.*

earthly pleasures, and then smother her with a stultifying affection. He passed his evenings in prayer, only to explode in anger when a desire was denied. He wrote sublime poems, but he had an insatiable appetite for carnal pleasures. These wild swings in temperament troubled Ratnavali, for as a devotee of Lord Rama she wanted her husband to embody only the noble qualities and thought of intimacy as a holy act to bring a new soul into the world.

"What do you say, Tulsidas? May I visit my family?" Ratnavali asked again.

"It seems that you have forgotten that a wife's happiness is with her husband and not with her parents."

"Can't you bear to be apart from me for just a few days?"

"Go! I'll be fine in your absence." Tulsidas made a show of indifference, all the while afraid that he would find the separation unbearable.

"Thank you, my husband! You are most understanding. I will be back home in three days."

Ratnavali packed a small bag while Tulsidas arranged for a carriage to take her to her parents' village, a small town on the other side of the Yamuna River. When the dreaded hour of parting arrived, Tulsidas bid her a perfunctory good-bye. He miserably watched the carriage until it disappeared, and then slammed the door of his house. Its crash echoed through the empty rooms, mocking his loneliness.

"I'll go to the temple or read the *Ramayana*," he thought, hoping to find the strength to endure this test. But no sooner had he resolved to do something worthwhile than he was undone by his broodings.

The very heavens seemed sympathetic to his mood: the sky put on a coat of leaden gray, and storm clouds gathered on the horizon. For several hours, he sat with chin in hand, watching the rain pattering in a puddle. At dinnertime, he forced himself to eat a few bites of the food Ratnavali had cooked, but it was tasteless. When it came time for bed, Tulsidas restlessly tossed and groaned. No matter how he reasoned with himself, no matter how fervently he prayed, his mind returned again and again to a single thought: Ratnavali.

"Oh! I cannot live without her, even for one night!" In a sudden rush, he threw off the blankets and put on his clothes. He would go to his in-laws' house, surprise Ratnavali, and take her in his arms. She would swoon, entranced by his romantic gesture of daring thunder and lightning.

As soon as he stepped outside, a cold rain pelted him. He lingered for a moment, wondering what kind of a man would travel several hours in a raging storm to gratify his lust. But desire took the whip to his reason, and he started off in a run down the sodden streets, his mind awhirl with thoughts of a passionate rendezvous.

"Lord, why do you thwart my plans?" Tulsidas cried as he reached the banks of the Yamuna River. In his agitation, he had forgotten that the Yamuna lay between him and fulfillment. A shaft of moonlight breaking through the clouds revealed a small shack and a boat tethered to a post. The village ferryman lived there, and he could help him.

Tulsidas raced to the hut, rapped on the door, and shouted, "Boatman, wake up! Boatman, wake up!"

"What is it that you want?" the boatman warily asked, distrustful of someone who would need his services on such a stormy night.

"You must ferry me across the Yamuna right now."

"Are you mad? The river is in flood. Come tomorrow, and I will take you then." The boatman closed the door, but Tulsidas was faster and forced himself into the house.

"What could be so important that you would risk crossing tonight?"

"That is none of your business," Tulsidas snapped as he surveyed the boatman's shack. In a corner, his children and wife slept under threadbare blankets. The cupboard was bare save a few vegetables. Rain dripped through the roof.

"Boatman, your children are cold, and your wife is worn from hard work. I will give you a month's pay if you ferry me across tonight. Think of all that you could buy for your family." He paused to gauge the boatman's response. "Or would you rather let them suffer because you lack the courage for the journey?"

"You are very cruel to put your offer this way, but I agree. Pay me now, for if we die tonight, I want my family to have a little money on which to live."

In his haste, Tulsidas had forgotten to bring his pouch, so he slid off his gold bracelet and handed it to the boatman, who nodded approvingly and readied himself for the passage. Two specters in the night, they ran to the riverbank and clambered into the boat. As soon as they launched the boat, white-tipped waves took hold of the skiff and tossed it from crest to crest, and a biting wind tore at the sails.

"Hurry, boatman. Hurry!"

"Keep quiet, and let me try to save our lives!"

A fast-moving current seized the boat and pulled it toward a churning abyss. Tulsidas clutched his seat, while the boatman struggled with the rudder. As they were about to go under, the sailor proved that his skill was equal to the river's rage, and they escaped the rapids. For another brutal hour, the boatman battled. When the hull scraped upon the far bank, the boatman threw his arms heavenward in thanks.

Tulsidas leapt onto land, and without stopping to look

back, raced toward town. Flashes of lightning illuminated the labyrinth of streets. No living thing stirred on such a stormy night. In the gloom, shadows on the walls turned sinister and stalked his imagination, and he panicked, believing the sound of his feet splashing in the puddles was that of a demon in pursuit.

At last he reached the doorstep of his in-laws' house. A final obstacle lay between him and his desire: The family was asleep, and he could not wake them up without causing a stir.

"I have not come this far to be deterred!" Sizing the house with the eyes of a thief, he saw that he could jump over the wall that surrounded the property, creep across the backyard, and climb up a vine that touched the window of the room in which Ratnavali slept. In a trice he did this and was inside the house.[1]

A moment of quiet overtook him as he watched his sleeping wife's chest rise and fall. His tender feelings were fleeting, however, and with a heart pounding in anticipation, he stealthily crept across the room, put his hand over Ratnavali's mouth, and gently shook her.

"Wake up, Ratnavali. I could not bear being apart, so I came to see you," Tulsidas said as he kissed her cheek. She gasped in terror until she realized that it was her husband who was by her side.

"How is it that you are here? It is pouring, and you are drenched. Did you cross the Yamuna in this weather? And how did you get into the house? Did you wake my parents? Oh, no, I see. . . ." Her voice trailed off as her eyes fell upon the open window.

"What does any of that matter? I am here now, and I love you!"

"You risked your life in this storm for passing pleasure? Tulsidas, you are a madman!" She pushed him away.

"You call me mad because I love you? Well, then I am mad." Tulsidas hoped his ardent avowal would convince his wife to be with him. Yet, shivering in his wet clothes, he could not help but wonder if he was insane, for had not the boatman called him mad, too?

"I do not profess to know the meaning of love, but this is not it. Love does not ask, and it does not want. It is not possessive or selfish. It is not demanding or self-serving. If this is your love for me, then we are both poor indeed." Ratnavali sorrowed for her tormented husband and their intertwined fate.

The two fell into a miserable silence. Though only a few feet apart, they were a world away. Tulsidas thought, "My wife is right. This is not love. This is lust. So what kind of a man am I? A hypocrite and a lecher. I have descended to the nadir of indignity."[2]

When Ratnavali spoke again, Tulsidas heard Lord Rama speaking through her. "If you have the same fire for God as you have for me, you will achieve salvation in this life."

These words were a gust of wind that blew away the great fog that had clouded his reason. "I must go now," Tulsidas finally said. Turning around, he left the room as he had entered.

As he walked through town, each step brought back another shameful memory of his past cravings. By the time he reached the river, the first light of the day streaked across the sky, and with it, he felt he had left his own darkness behind.

LORD GANESHA
GOD OF NEW BEGINNINGS

Most worship services in India begin with a brief invocation to Ganesha, the elephant-headed god who is the remover of obstacles and the source of good luck. Because of his ausipiciousness he is prayed to by the devotee at the start of a new undertaking.

CHAPTER TWENTY-THREE

Forgiveness

One should forgive, under any injury. It hath been said that the continuation of the species is due to man being forgiving. Forgiveness is holiness; by forgiveness the universe is held together. Forgiveness is the might of the mighty; forgiveness is sacrifice; forgiveness is quiet of mind.

—THE MAHABHARATA

THE MIGHT OF THE MIGHTY ⁊

The empire of Abdul Hasan Tanashah stretched a thousand miles, from the capital of Hyderabad in the Deccan Plateau to the provincial town of Bhadrachalam on the banks of the river Godavari. Not content to lord over his subjects, Tanashah imposed the Jaziya tax, a harsh penalty meant to force Hindus to convert to Islam. While Nizams[1] in the past had used the sword to force religious conversions, Tanashah's methods were subtler and hence far more effective in undermining the Sanatana Dharma.[2]

Gopanna (1620–1688? C.E.) was born in Nelakondapalli, a small village located in Andhra Pradesh. The chief events associated with his life are told in this story. He is also remembered for composing a number of devotional songs to Rama. Two translations are included in the narrative.

One of the Nizam's servants was Gopanna, a man who found himself in the most paradoxical of positions. He served as the Nizam's tax collector of Bhadrachalam and enforced the Jaziya tax, yet he was a devout Hindu who donated much of his salary to feed the poor in the name of Sri Rama. The incompatibility between his duties and his convictions tormented him, and he prayed year after year for the Lord's guidance.

During meditation one evening, Sri Rama came. "My Son, the foundations of my temple are cracked, and its pillars are crumbling. Build for me a new temple where my devotees can gather for worship, and I promise you salvation."

Gopanna answered, "My Father, whatever you ask of me I will do, even though I am a poor government official. If need be, I shall give you my blood to fulfill your command."

Early the next morning, Gopanna resolved to go from door to door until he had raised the necessary funds. "Dear neighbor," he began each time he asked for a donation, "I've had a vision of Sri Rama, and he asked me to build a temple for him. Will you help me?"

"You cause stir enough by feeding the poor in Rama's name. If Tanashah should find out your plans, we'll all be hanged," one spoke in reply.

Another said, "I've had a vision, too, in which I was told not to donate my hard-earned money to tax collectors."

At the end of a day of endless rejections, he stood before the last house, fervently praying for a miracle. "How dare you ask me for a contribution when you tax me for being a Hindu? Your master, Tanashah, must be pleased that he has such spineless lackeys to do his bidding!"

Gopanna blanched at the man's accusation. He thought, "For years I have tried to convince myself that I was just a dutiful government official. But now I see that I have been a traitor to my own people. This Jaziya tax has made me rich, but it has reduced my brothers and sisters to poverty and desperation. Every rupee I have taken counts as a sin against me. How will I ever redeem my numberless wrongs?"

With these thoughts churning in his mind, Gopanna aimlessly walked for many hours. When he returned to his home in the evening, he threw himself before his altar.

"Father, now I understand why you asked me to build the temple. But I do not have the means to do this. So I will commit the smaller sin of keeping a portion of the Nizam's taxes for the higher purpose of building a temple for all. Since the accountants at the royal treasury trust me, they will believe that revenues have decreased. And by the time they find out what I have done, I will have built the temple and will be ready to accept the consequences."

Soon Gopanna hoarded enough to erect a beautiful shrine in Bhadrachalam. Its stately gopurams could be seen from miles away, and it gave those wavering in faith the courage to openly pray again.[3]

When word finally came to Tanashah that a Hindu house of worship had been built with his money, he shook with rage and sent a company of soldiers to arrest Gopanna. They tied his wrists, bound him to horses, and dragged him through the streets so that all would see how the Nizam dealt with traitors and thieves.

"How dare you use my gold to build a temple for your god?" The Nizam towered over the bloodied tax collector.

"I followed Sri Rama's command." Gopanna's guileless reply brought a crash of contemptuous laughter from the court.

"So that is your defense?" Tanashah sneered. "Lest my tax

collectors think they can steal from the royal treasury with impunity, I will make an example of you. I condemn you to Golconda Fort for twelve years or until the time you are able to repay what you have stolen."

Many were condemned to the dungeons of Golconda, but few lived to tell of their imprisonment.

"Please forgive me! I have served you faithfully for many years. Can you not pardon this one offense?"

"There is no mercy in me for you," the Nizam smiled. "Get him out of my sight before I impose a harsher sentence!"

Golconda's iron doors groaned open in sadistic welcome. Down flights of stairs, down narrow passageways, down, down, Gopanna was dragged into a miserable world of pitiful moans and abrupt shrieks, dank corners and stygian darkness. A putrid stench of decay and disease nauseated him.

"What man could survive twelve years of this?" Gopanna gasped as he saw a prisoner stumble under the whip of a grinning guard. He felt as if the sun had gone out of his life.

"Welcome to your new home. May you rot in it!" The soldier shoved him into a cavelike cell. In the grinding of the heavy gates behind him, Gopanna heard the finality of his sentence.

He fell to the floor and began to pray. "Lord, why have you not saved me from this? You promised me final freedom but have instead put me in this horrible prison. Now it is good-bye sun, good-bye air, good-bye moon."

Golconda quickly became a crucible of suffering for Gopanna. Only by his tortures was he able to measure time. He awoke every day to the screams of his fellow prisoners, which soon became his own as soldiers put him to the rack, and he went to bed at night to a lullaby of insults and threats. With no light to tell morning from evening and no companion other than the gnawing pain of slow starvation, his days passed in a maddening monotony that was broken only by the beatings of prison guards.

Years passed, and according to Gopanna's reckoning, he had served his sentence. Now that the Lord had forsaken him, he accused, "I had taxed your devotees for their faith, and in my hour of trial, Father, you tax mine." As the guards thrashed him, he sung out in bitterness:

> Sri Rama, I had an emerald pendant made for your
>   brother, Bharata.
> I had a gold waistband made for your brother,
>   Sathrughna.
> I had a pearl necklace made for your brother,
>   Lakshmana.
> I had a tamarind-leaf pendant made for your wife, Sita.
> You all enjoy wearing my jewels.
> But who will pay for this huge debt?
> I'm suffering for your sake, oh, God!

But then he recanted:

> My God, have I been rude to you before?
> I cannot endure this flogging anymore.
> Out of frustration I chided you.
> O savior of your devotees, oh, Sri Rama,
> Kindly lead your devotee safely to your presence.

Outside Golconda, life went on. Tanashah grew richer, more and more pilgrims gathered at the temple in Bhadrachalam, and the river Godavari continued to flow. Inside Golconda, Gopanna waged war against the darkness by con-

AUM

The syllable OM, also called *pranava*, is the most sacred mystic symbol of Hinduism. "The goal which all Vedas declare, which all austerities aim at, and which humans who lead a life of continence desire . . . it is OM. This syllable OM is indeed Brahman." (Katha Upanishad, I, II, 15–17) stantly chanting Rama's name. After praying until he thought his heart would break, his faith began to weaken, and a cancerous doubt spread into his soul.

"I promised that I would give my life to build your temple, and you have taken me at my word," Gopanna said after bleeding under the lash of the whip. "Father, now you don't need to send soldiers to punish me anymore, for I offer you my blood freely."

Putting his hand to the rough wall, he started scratching a picture of Sri Rama. Fingernail after fingernail fell off and blood trickled to the floor as he cut the image in stone. When he finished, he lay on the freezing floor, his heart barely beating, his mind flitting between this world and the next. The sound of approaching feet broke his passion.

"Gopanna of Bhadrachalam?" The cell door opened and in the threshold stood an imperious figure flanked by soldiers.

"It is I," Gopanna mumbled, certain that his final hour was at hand.

"You may leave us now." It was Tanashah who spoke these words to his guards. He entered the cell and stifled a gasp as he beheld his prisoner. Gopanna was a spectral figure, aged, emaciated, and scarred from countless floggings. As soon as the door closed, Tanashah fell to his knees. "Gopanna! You must forgive me! I am in terror of your gods!

"What do you mean?" Gopanna looked in bewilderment at the Nizam.

"Today, two men of royal bearing appeared at my court. One was of fair complexion and respectful toward his elder companion, who was tall and dark and had a most striking face. They carried with them bows and arrows, and though clearly formidable warriors, they seemed foremost to be men of peace." What the Nizam did not say was that he knew these two princes were far greater men than he.

"Intimate with your plight, they carried with them the exact amount in gold and jewels you took from the royal treasury and repaid your debt. As the conditions of your release had been met, they insisted that I free you immediately." Feeling like the lowliest of foot soldiers next to these kingly figures, Tanashah had instantly obeyed their order.

"Sri Rama and Lakshmana!"[4]

"I feared it was the gods for whom you built the temple, and I am in terror to know that it is indeed so. You must forgive me. Can you not find a little mercy in yourself for me?"

Gopanna heard in the Nizam's words the same appeal for forgiveness he himself had made twelve years ago. He had asked for clemency, and it had been denied, and because of that, he had suffered excruciatingly. Now he was presented with an opportunity to let Tanashah languish. But he knew that he had been the beneficiary of the Lord's unmerited mercy, and he understood how the Master Novelist wanted this strange tale to end.

"If my Rama has appeared to you, that means he loves you, and you are my brother disciple. As my Father forgave my many sins by paying my debt to you, I forgive you for all that has passed between us."

Upon uttering these words the veils of darkness fell away, and all the events of his life, enigmatic and opaque until now, became lucent. In this handiwork of Sri Rama, Gopanna saw that his deliverance had come disguised as suffering and that through the building of the temple he had upheld the Sanatana Dharma and that many souls had come nearer to God because of this. A divine joy suddenly engulfed his heart, and the horrors of many years counted as nothing next to the cascades of love that swept over him.

"Such magnanimity and compassion are only possible if a man is touched by God," said a relieved Tanashah as he looked at the tax collector about whose face a new light danced. "I order your immediate release and restore you to your former position as tax collector, should you condescend to accept it. I also place the temple in your care and declare that my descendants henceforth shall make yearly offerings to atone for my sins. What do you say?"

"All I ask is that you let me return home," Gopanna smiled, for liberation was at hand, and there was nothing more to want.

Sweet so sweet did the air taste, as he drew his first breath outside of Golconda. As Gopanna hurried back to Bhadrachalam, he began to sing:

> I spell death to the messengers of death itself: heartily
>   believe that brother!
> The sins of countless incarnations are all dissolved in
>   this life.
> This is the last life.
> There will be no more rebirths: that is the truth!
> In my heart, I have complete faith that is the truth![5]

CHAPTER TWENTY-FOUR

Freedom from Hate

Wrath springs only from thwarted desires.

—SWAMI SRI YUKTESWAR,
AUTOBIOGRAPHY OF A YOGI

UPASENA'S LAST BREATH

"Lift up this body and carry it outside before it is scattered like a fistful of chaff!"[1] The venerable Upasena's abrupt exclamation broke the meditative silence of his fellow monks in their forest grotto.

"What troubles you, my friend?" asked Sariputta, alarmed by the sudden cry.

A sibilant sound caught the attention of Sariputta, and he froze in terror at the sight of a cobra slithering out of the cave. The other monks jumped up and began shouting and running about in fear and confusion. When they looked at Upasena, they saw two trickles of blood on his ankle marking the place where the snake had left its fatal bite.

"Are you all right?"

"Somebody get some water! Get a bandage!"

Upasena was a Buddhist monk who probably lived around 300 B.C.E. The following story was recorded in the holy text, the Samyutta Nikaya, sometime around 100 B.C.E.

"It is of no use," Upasena said. "The medicine man lives too far away to get an antidote."

"What a cruel fate for our great master to die by a vile reptile!" grieved a young monk as he picked up a stick with the intent of smashing the creature's head. For he, like all the other brothers, deeply revered the gentle and wise Upasena.

"Let us kill the snake!" said another young monk, who thought of Upasena like a father.

"Forget your anger. Forget the creature," Upasena cried again, his breath now labored from the spreading poison.

"How can you say that? It has robbed you of your life!" said Sariputta, weeping for the loss of a dear friend who had been with him since he had entered the order.

"Why would I hate the agent that caused the end of this form? Where there is no desire, there can be no attachment to the body. Where there is no attachment to the body, life and death are the same. I am not the eye, I am not the ear, I am not this nose, I am not the mind."

The monks looked at the dying man in admiration. They knew all along that Upasena was of great spiritual stature, but hearing him use his last breath to teach them about the impermanence of life and the true nature of things was proof that Upasena was no longer identified with the flesh and hence beyond hatred and all the other fetters that bind man.

The snake was allowed to go unharmed as the monks gently lifted up their teacher and brought him out into the cool night air. Sariputta put Upasena's head in his lap and held his friend. Upasena shuddered one last time and his body seemed to scatter like a fistful of chaff tossed into the wind.

TWENTY FIVE

Absence of Conceit

Everyone is holy company, every place is holy ground, and every act is sacred practice.

—BO LOZOFF, *SACRED AMERICA*

ADI SANKARA AND
THE CHANDALA[I]

In the holy city of Varanasi, at the edge of the river Ganges, lived a chandala, one who had the gruesome task of feeding corpses into crematory fires.

The chandala was as ugly as his work was vile. A snoutlike nose and buckteeth peeped through a wild and unkempt

---

Sankara (788–820? C.E.) is widely considered to be one of India's greatest and most important saints and scholars. Born in a time of chaos and unrest when the Hindu faith had fragmented into numerous cults, was riddled with caste prejudices, and was on the verge of collapse, Sankara rejuvenated Hinduism through his philosophical discourses, writings, and the establishment of the Swami order, with four maths (monasteries) in the four corners of India.

Sankara's commentaries on the Upanishads, the Gita, and his many other devotional compositions contributed to a body of knowledge that came to be the fountainhead of modern Hindu thought. Venerable nineteenth- and twentieth-century Indian masters, including Sri Ramakrishna, Swami Vivekananda, Paramahansa Yogananda, Sri Aurobindo, Ramana Maharshi, and Maharshi Mahesh Yogi, owe their intellectual, spiritual, and sometimes their monastic allegiance to Adi Sankara.

beard. His body was blackened with soot, his fingernails were caked with grime and blood, and his leather sash was stained with foul secretions. With hunched back, gangly arms, and speech more grunts than words, he seemed more animal than man.

It was a miserable existence for the chandala. His only companions were a pack of mangy dogs that nipped at his legs and incessantly yapped to get his attention. And when he fell asleep at night, his dreams were of crematory fires and of corpses whose limbs jerked from the intense heat of the burning logs as if they were alive.

Despised by all, the chandala despised himself. Convinced that he was unworthy to look upon this world, he never turned his eyes from his work. Yet, today, he sat and stared at a ghat upstream that was used by pilgrims for their morning devotions.

A large retinue of swamis had just finished their ablutions and were making their way toward him. Such a band of radiant monks had never passed this way before. As they neared, the chandala ran to the edge of the crematory grounds and peered over the fence.

He heard one young monk say, "I think Master Sankara's greatest accomplishment was defeating the theologian Mandana Mishra and the pundits of Varanasi in debate. By doing so, he has started to purge the Sanatana Dharma of much superstition, idolatry, and cultism."

"I say Master Sankara's most important achievement was his commentaries on the Upanishads.[2] Generations of devotees will find guidance in these profound works," stated a second monk.

"No," said a third. "It is how he taught the direct way to the Mother of Creation is the path of childlike devotion."

Though the chandala did not fully understand what the monks said, he somehow knew that their words were important and true. He eagerly waited to see the one they so reverentially talked about, and a moment later, the Teacher appeared.

The chandala had never seen such a beatific-looking man. His smile was playful yet compassionate, and his movements were graceful and serene. Most of all, his bewitching black eyes radiated a tremendous power and love.

As if charmed by a magical spell, the chandala staggered out of the crematory ghat and approached Sankara, the dogs still barking at his heels. He was not sure what he wanted from the sage, though he would have given up all that was his for a word of encouragement or a kindly glance.

"What are you doing, chandala?" shouted a zealous devotee as he shooed away the dogs. "How dare you approach Master Sankara?"

The chandala looked with hope at the great master, but he was met with an annoyed scowl.

"Please, not now. I am in a hurry to get to a symposium," said Sankara.

The spell of enchantment snapped, and the chandala remembered that he was only the keeper of the dead and the most reviled of men. Reproaching himself for foolishly hoping that his life might be something other than bitterness and toil, he dejectedly walked back to the smoldering pyres.

That night, Sankara found his mind troubled. During meditation, his thoughts kept returning to the ghat and the chandala. Suddenly he knew that he had failed a test and berated himself for believing that a scholarly debate was more important than tending to the sincere aspiration of a neglected man, and he judged himself to be guilty of the sin of conceit.[3]

When dawn broke, Sankara hurried down to the river and quickly said his prayers. To his disciples' surprise, instead of going to the temple, he walked to the crematory ghat and called for the chandala. Timid and confused, the chandala appeared at the gate.

Sankara gently spoke, "Friend, I did a great injustice to you yesterday. By dismissing you, I had forgotten that we are all equal before God. Now I want to make amends. Please allow me to cook your meal, clean your hut, and tend your fires today. Serving you in this way will be my penance and my peace."

Looking at the tender of fires, Sankara felt that he was speaking to the Lord himself who had taken a repugnant form to test the humility of his devotee. As Sankara walked toward the crematorium, Padmapada, a senior disciple, rushed forward to remind the Master of the many duties of the day. Sankara brushed him aside, and to the shock of all present, continued toward the ghat. The chandala opened the gate with a beautiful smile and welcomed his guest as if he were greeting an old friend after a long separation.

GODDESS DURGA

Durga is one of the most widely revered deities in the Hindu religion. Her name literally means "fort," and implies that the Divine Mother protects all her children who take refuge in Her from evil, just as a castle protects one from enemies.

CHAPTER TWENTY-SIX

Patience

In the valley of sorrow
A thousand years or till tomorrow
But I'll wait to see you
You, You, just You
—PARAMAHANSA YOGANANDA,
COSMIC CHANTS

NANDANAR WAITS FOR LORD NATARAJA[1]

Pausing from his eternal dance of creation and annihilation, Lord Nataraja looked down on the world and watched one of his devotees pass from earth into the land of forgetfulness called death and then incarnate again as a little boy named Nandanar.

Born sometime between 660 and 840 C.E. into an untouchable family, Nandanar lived in the town of Adanur located in the North Arcot district of modern Tamil Nadu. He was a farm hand and was probably responsible for the "unclean" and hence shameful task of transporting animal carcasses to town to be made into drums and other musical instruments.

His great devotion to Lord Nataraja won him a place in the Periyapurana, *a noted scripture recounting the lives of the sixty-three Nayanar saints—men and women who were perfect devotees of Lord Siva. The heroic strivings of Nandanar's life have captivated biographers and poets for centuries.*

The child had lived many virtuous lives and was on the cusp of liberation, but because he had not yet learned patience, he was born into impoverished and trying circumstances. Taking pity on his devotee, Nataraja, the keeper of time and watcher of souls, guided Nandanar by whispering inspirations in his devotee's heart.

"Hello playmate! Do you remember me? You forsook our great cosmic game of shooting stars across the sky and spinning galaxies on fingertips to instead crawl on a ball of mud and play with tawdry trinkets. Wouldn't you rather come back to your true home beyond boundless space?"

Nandanar abruptly stopped playing in the street with his companions, put down his toys, looked about, and saw for the first time that he was surrounded by squalor. The stench from the village tanneries, a pack of dogs fighting over a pile of chicken bones, the foul language of two arguing neighbors, and his own unwashed body, all unnoticed before now, made him feel tainted.

"I don't like it here at all. This place frightens me. What can I do to return home?" Nandanar scampered off to the little mud hut where he lived with his grandmother and tearfully asked her to explain what had happened.

"For a long time I had kept these things from you, but you are now old enough to understand," his grandmother spoke. "We are untouchables. You have entered into this life with nothing, you will have nothing, and you will leave with nothing. Through no fault of your own, all will despise you. When you are too weak to work, you will be discarded like an old horse left to die in the fields, and when you're dead, no priest will come to bless your body. Only God can help us, and we can reach him by worshiping Nataraja, just as the Nayanar saints of Chidambaram[2] did."

So Nandanar shaped out of clay a likeness of Nataraja, hoping that it would whisk him away to a fairer land. Though he loved the statue as the parents he no longer had, it never spoke to him. His companions, seeing that he had lost interest in playing, taunted him and then abandoned him, and Nandanar passed the rest of his childhood friendless.

"Whether you walk alone or with others, in the end, you must make the final crossing by yourself. In truth, though, I ever remain by your side. All will be yours in time if you continue with your efforts," Nataraja encouragingly whispered in the youth's heart after he had prayed unceasingly for several years.

"I know why you haven't answered!" Nandanar clapped his hands in excitement. "I don't pray correctly like the priests. Perhaps if I do as they do, I, too, will be able to speak with you."

So every morning before dawn, Nandanar made his way to the river in the darkness. Shivering in the cold, he hid in a bluff, waiting for the priests to arrive. When they turned east toward the rising sun, so did Nandanar. When they dipped in the river intoning mantras, likewise did he, making up words that struck his imagination as sacred. All this brought him a little peace but not the end he sought.

One day some villagers espied him standing half-immersed in the river, mumbling with an earnest expression on his face. "Look at that pariah pretending to be a Brahmin! He is mocking our faith, and for that we should beat him."

Tiptoeing to the water's edge, they waited until Nandanar took his next dip and then rushed forward, grabbed his arms, and tried to drown him. When his flailing grew weak, they dragged him onto the shore and thrashed him until his breath seemed to cease. Nandanar crawled to his hut and lay there for weeks in a deathlike delirium. No good soul came in response to his cries.

"My Lord, my prayers must displease you, but I have not had any training in mantras, so I come to you the only way I know. Give me strength to continue, for the blows of the world are greater than I can bear. I am a man who belongs nowhere and to no one—a leather worker hated by my fellow laborers for wanting God and a devotee despised by everyone else for tanning animal skins for a living"

"My son! I suffer with you like a mother for her child. But remember that your true nature is not flesh and bones. This life is just a game, a maze of earthly existence that confounds all but the most determined of seekers. I will tell you a shortcut: Work for me; use your trade and talents in my service."

Nandanar smiled with an inspiration. "Now I know what I should do! Since you hold a drum in your hand, you must like mridangams.[3] I will make you a set as a present."

To purchase the finest woods and skins, Nandanar stopped buying food and hoarded his wages so that he could make a beautiful offering to Nataraja. With loving care he stretched and tanned the leather and carved and polished the wood. By the time he had crafted a perfect set, he was wasted from hunger. Walking in a weakened state to the temple of Adanur, he implored the Lord to allow him one glimpse of the statue in the shrine.

Nandanar gave the mridangams to a priest, who, surprised that a lowly laborer could produce something so beautiful, offered a begrudging compliment. "What a fine tone these drums have! We shall play them during temple services. You may go now, and consider my words to be your blessings."

"Sir, can I please have a *darshan*[4] of Lord Nataraja this once? I have gone a week without food to make these."

The priest glowered in reply, and Nandanar walked away with his head bowed.

"As a child, I worshiped your likeness but you remained

mute. As a youth, I imitated the priests and was beaten for it.
As a man, I have used my hands in your service, and still that
has not pleased you. Your silence is too much to bear."

"To feel my unconditional love, you must surrender unconditionally, trusting that your greatest happiness lies in following my will. Press on knowing that you are ever moving toward me."

One year when there was no work to be found in the tannery, Nandanar indentured himself to Subramanya, the avaricious landlord of Adanur. Subramanya worked his field hands from morning until night and Nandanar could hardly stay awake to say his evening prayers.

After toiling in the fields on this day, Nandanar walked through a grove, dejected that his many years of striving had been fruitless. Just when he was about to return home, a mellifluous voice coming through the trees caught his attention. An elderly teacher was speaking to a group of young men. "Chidambaram is the holiest city in the world. In the temple there stands the most resplendent image of Lord Nataraja. Anyone who has a darshan will be assured of liberation."

"Chidambaram!" Nandanar exclaimed in recognition. Childhood memories of his grandmother telling him about the holy city and its Nayanar saints came rushing back to his recollection. In the sage's words, Nandanar heard an immense promise of many lifetimes that was soon to be redeemed, and he hurried to Subramanya.

"You want to go to Chidambaram? Have you forgotten that you are a serf forbidden to enter a temple?" Subramanya ridiculed. Struck by his field hand's strange fervor, the landlord calculated how he could take advantage of it to his own end. "I will strike a bargain with you. If you can harvest this rice field without anyone's help by nightfall, I will let you go to Chidambaram. But if you fail, you must agree to become my slave for life."

The rice field stretched endlessly. It would take two or three men feverishly working all day to complete the harvest. Nandanar picked up the scythe and thought, "I have lived my life as a slave and will die as a slave. But if I win today, bliss awaits me in Chidambaram." Meanwhile, Subramanya exulted that he would own a new servant at nightfall.

Once in the field, Nandanar chanted with every swing of his scythe, "I am going to Chidambaram! I am going to Chidambaram!"[5] As he worked, all the troubles, pains, and the frustrated yearnings of his life became fuel for his devotional fervor. It consumed his body, and he knew that his heart would break under the strain at this pace.

In the heat of the midday, when the fields became so hot that even the dogs took shelter and the world seemed without life, Nandanar worked on without respite, beads of perspiration mingling with teardrops. Just as he was about to faint, the sound of the wind came upon him, and a cool gust took hold of his mind. A celestial fire coursed through his veins, and he felt his consciousness ripple through the vast expanses of grass, sweep through the town of Adanur, down dusty highways to Chidambaram, and then spread out to the horizon in endless directions. As suddenly as the epiphany came, it vanished.

When the last embers of the day were dying, there came a knock on Subramanya's door. Nandanar stood before him, wearing a radiant smile.

"How is it that you have finished?" Subramanya was aghast. Before he could speak again, Nandanar turned and left.

Walking many days without stopping, for none would offer conveyance to an untouchable, he finally arrived at

Chidambaram. For weeks, he kept a vigil in front of the western gopuram, waiting for Lord Nataraja to arrange a miracle that would allow him to enter the temple, but none was forthcoming.

"Time is fleeting, death nears, and still I am denied the one thing for which I have lived," Nandanar thought, knowing that his lifeblood had been consumed by the years of hard labor and deprivations, the exertions in the field, and the rigors of his recent journey.

"If I am omnipresent, am I not in you and everyone and everything? Look for me in others, feel me in their sorrows and joys, and then it will not matter where I place you."

Nandanar patiently waited, his frail, motionless body covered in rags, his heart beating feebly. Summoning the last of his strength, he fixed his attention unwaveringly on the Lord of Chidambaram. He no longer felt a need to enter the temple, for now he could cross the threshold by being one with the hearts of passing pilgrims. In an old man, he prayed for healing from illness. In a newly married couple, he dreamed of a happy life. In a merchant, he desired continued prosperity. In a swami, he sought the Lord for himself. Many times and in many ways Nandanar made his pilgrimage, but to those who passed him by he was a wretched peasant.

On the seventh week of his vigil there came a procession of scholars. As Nandanar watched them pass into the temple, he could see their innermost thoughts. Many among them were mired in fruitless theological musings and content with vain speculations, while Nandanar, feeling the Lord's love pulsating in every atom, was moved to compassion for them.

"There is nothing more to want and nothing more to be

gained. Though I may never see you with human eyes, I am content."

"Our game is nearing an end. Just a few more steps and you will be out of the Cosmic Maze to discover that you are bliss cloaked in dreams of flesh."

The next morning, Nandanar awoke to see the scholars spilling out of the temple. They subjected every man to their anxious scrutiny exclaiming, "Is it him?" "No him!" "Come this way!"

"He is the one!" an elderly sage shouted as he pointed to Nandanar. All the scholars rushed over to him. "Friend, last night each one of us was graced by a vision in which the Lord told us that His devotee is sleeping in tattered clothes outside the western gopuram. You are the one He commanded us to bring into the temple."

To the sound of Vedic hymns and temple bells, Nandanar was led like an honored guest through the massive gate and into the temple precincts. As he was ushered into the sanctum sanctorum, the noise and dust of the street disappeared in a profound stillness.

There on a platform stood Nataraja, one foot gracefully upraised, the other firmly planted on a dwarf blinded by maya. One hand held a two-sided drum; fire leaped from the palm of another; a third made a sign that he would help in the fight against darkness and evil; and a fourth pointed downward to show the way to escape from the wheel of reincarnation. A ring of fire was behind him, and a crescent moon floated in his matted hair. Dressed in silks of the most exquisite design, he was adorned with bangles, bracelets, and necklaces of rubies, sapphires, and emeralds. On top of his head lay a gold and diamond crown of dazzling radiance.

"Oh, oh, after all these years . . . and now our long

separation is over." Nandanar fell prostrate before the statue as a torrent of love surged through him. "You are more beautiful, tender, loving than I ever imagined."

At the threshold where time met eternity, Nataraja resumed his cosmic dance of creation and annihilation. As the statue[6] came to life, Nandanar heard from Nataraja's drum the roar of Aum, the sound that formed the universe, held the planets in orderly procession and pumped life into the hearts of all living things. From his hand, solar systems and galaxies took birth, came of age, and then dissolved.

It filled Nandanar with awe to behold a Lord for whom making universes was child's play but whose eyes radiated unconditional, everlasting love for his smallest creation. Bathed in an indescribable bliss, he felt the last cords of desire unravel, and his soul leaped like a spark to commingle in the Cosmic Fire. In a blink of an eye for Nataraja, the life of Nandanar had passed.

"Stop singing, please! I beg of you, stop singing!" the elderly scholar's voice rose above the chanting of the pilgrims. Nandanar lay lifeless on the floor. "What joy, what joy, what joy! Our friend has finally escaped from the thralldom of delusive seeming. Though he had to wait until the last minute of the last day of his life, he is finally free!"

"I did not put you through your trials to punish you but to make our reunion that much sweeter. Do you now understand, my son?" Lord Nataraja whispered to Nandanar as he embraced him in arms of celestial light.

NATARAJA

Nataraja (literally, "Lord of the Dance") is a form of Siva, and can be found in many temples throughout South India. The image represents the triune aspects of the cycle of life: Creation, as shown by the drum from which emanates the original vibration that formed this universe; Preservation, as symbolized by his right hand making the gesture of the *abhaya mudra* (protection); and Destruction, by the fire springing from the left hand.

NOTES

Introduction

1. *Wisdom's Blossoms* consists of stories from the oral tradition that should be read as historical fiction and not as unassailable fact. Sunil Gangopadhyay, the noted Bengali novelist, writes, "History is a record of palpable facts. Fiction is not. The fiction writer, even when depicting historical truth, has to invest it with the light of his imagination" (in *Those Days*, trans. Aruna Chakravarti [New Delhi, India: Penguin Books, 1997], p. ix). Taking a similar approach, we have imbued the narratives with our imagination wherever appropriate, while ascertaining historical fact whenever possible.

2. Paramahansa Yogananda, *God Talks with Arjuna: The Bhagavad Gita* (Los Angeles: Self-Realization Fellowship, 1996), p. 955.

Chapter 1: Upagupta and the Courtesan

1. *Sutras* are spiritual principles or discourses written in Sanskrit and/or Pali.

2. Happiness for the good man—
   Happiness now, happiness later
   Happiness in this world and the next.
   His deeds breed happiness, and he rejoices.

From *The Dhammapada,* trans. P. Lal (New York: Noonday Press, 1967), p. 41.

3. "One who has gone beyond the muddy road, this hard-going routine delusion, the meditative one who has crossed over, transcended, free from lust, without a doubt, ungrasping, perfectly serene, is one that I call priestly." From Thomas Cleary, *Dhammapada: The Sayings of Buddha* (New York: Bantam Wisdom Editions, 1995), p. 132.

The story of Upagupta has a number of variations, probably because it is so old, and most are not satisfying. For example, one scholarly work, *The Legend and Cult of Upagupta,* has Upagupta meeting Vasavadatta only once before he was a monk. In this version, Vasavadatta sends her servant to buy perfumes from Upagupta's shop. After hearing that the young man is both attractive and generous, Vasavadatta becomes interested in Upagupta and invites him to "pursue pleasure." He declines. At this time, Vasavadatta has a lover. A second lover enters the scene, and she tries to have her first lover killed so she can elope with her new interest. Her plan is uncovered, and as punishment, her hands, feet, nose, and ears are cut off. Upagupta comes to her at this juncture, not to fulfill his desires, as she mistakenly believes, but to tend to her injuries.

There are other renditions of this story as in Ksemendra's *Avadaanakalpalataa Sutra* and in the *Divyaavadaana Sutra.* We chose our version because it was more compelling than the scholarly account cited here, and it was the one that Sarat grew up hearing.

Chapter 2: Sitamma Feeds the Poor

1. In the Hindu tradition, dying in Varanasi is considered to be auspicious because the soul is ushered into the kingdom of God, assuring that there are no further rebirths.

Chapter 3: Tegh Bahadur Helps His Hindu Brothers

1. Aurangzeb's father was Shah Jahan, the builder of the Taj Mahal. Aurangzeb imprisoned him in a cell where he could see it in the distance. It is said that he spent his last days a brokenhearted man, wistfully looking at the mausoleum in which his wife was buried.

2. Guru Gobind Singh was the tenth and last in the line of the Sikh gurus. In order to defend India from constant external aggressions, he transformed the Sikh religion into a martial faith.

3. The word *Dharma* has a number of connotations: "duty," "faith," "justice," and "natural law" are some of them. In Pali, it is *Dhamma*.

4. At the time of this story, Hinduism and Sikhism were so intermingled that they might not have been seen as distinct faiths. It was in the intervening centuries that Sikhism developed its own religious identity.

5. Tegh Bahadur's death was not in vain. His son raised an army, and the Sikhs, along with the Rajputs, took up arms against the Mughals. Their rebellion weakened Aurangzeb's hold on India and marked the beginning of the demise of the Mughal Empire.

Chapter 4: The Weaver, the Fakir, and the Pig

1. A Muslim religious mendicant.

2. *Guru* is the washer man, the disciple is the cloth
   The name of God liken to the soap
   Wash the mind on foundation firm
   To realize the glow of Truth

   —Kabir

From *Bijak Vani* (Bombay, India: Baharamji Phirojashaha Madan, 1810).

Chapter 5: The Wedding Feast That Never Was

1. One of the central tenets of the Jain religion is *ahimsa*—nonviolence toward any living creature. This injunction is taken so

seriously that Jain monks wear masks over their mouths so they
do not inhale any living things, and some sweep the ground before them when they walk to make sure they do not step on an
insect or even seeds. Householders show a similar respect for all
life. Ahimsa is also more than a physical act; it means to harbor
no negative or harmful thoughts toward others.

Chapter 6: The Buddha and the Bandit

1. *Ahimsaka* means "one who does no harm." *Angulimala* means
"finger garland."

2. Taxila, also known as Takshasila, whose ruins are located in
present-day Pakistan, was a renowned university in the pre-
Christian era. Students from all over the world gathered there to
study philosophy, engineering, astronomy, medicine, languages,
and the arts.

3. Guru-dakshina means an offering to the guru in appreciation
for his having imparted temporal and spiritual knowledge.
Students were expected to fulfill the Guru-dakshina on comple-
tion of their training, and a great stigma was attached to those who
refused to comply.

4. *Dhammapada: The Sayings of Buddha*, p. 56.

5. The prince Siddhartha Gautama, who later became the
Buddha, belonged to the royal lineage of the Sakyas. Muni is one
who engages in austerities, often keeping "mouna," or silence.
Therefore, Sakya Muni is another name for the Buddha.

6. Sometime after this story, Angulimala was reportedly attacked by
the townspeople, some of whom sought revenge for their lost ones
and some who still believed he was unreformed. The wounds proved
fatal, but before he died, he was able to reach the Buddha and died
in his lap. After his death, several monks asked where Angulimala was
to be reborn. The Buddha replied that he had achieved final liberation. When the monks expressed disbelief, the Buddha remarked

that Angulimala had freed himself by his sincere and faithful practice of the Dhamma. Because of his redemption, many human rights activists, civil libertarians, and prison reformers cite the story as proof that even the most degenerate of men can be rehabilitated. Thus, they conclude that capital punishment should be abolished.

Chapter 7: The Man Who Spat on a Saint

1. In some versions of this story (Savittribai Khanolkar, *Saints of Maharashtra* [Bombay, India: Bharatiya Vidya Bhavan, 1978], p. 112), the antagonist is a young Muslim man who sought to insult Eknath, who at that time was a widely venerated Hindu saint.

2. *Ghats* are steps leading down to a river.

Chapter 8: Two Cloths

1. *Digambara* means "sky-clad."

2. "Just as an individual forsaking dilapidated raiment dons new clothes, so the body encased soul, relinquishing decayed bodily habitations, enters others that are new." From *God Talks with Arjuna: The Bhagavad-Gita*, p. 217.

"No weapon can pierce the soul; no fire can burn it; no water can moisten it; nor can any wind wither it." From *God Talks with Arjuna: The Bhagavad-Gita*, p. 221. In Lalla's own words:

> Let them jeer or cheer me;
> Let anybody says what he likes;
> Let good persons worship me with flowers;
> What can any one of them gain I being pure?

> If the world talks ill of me
> My heart shall harbor no ill will:
> If I am a true worshipper of God
> Can ashes leave a stain on a mirror?

From P. N. Kaul Bamzai, *Forerunner of Medieval Mystics* (Kashmir, India: Koshur Samachar, 2000), p. 2.

Chapter 10: To the Lover Thou Art Love

1. Lord Krishna, the eighth incarnation of Lord Vishnu, was raised in Brindaban by his adoptive parents, Yashoda and Nanda. His childhood playmates were *gopas* (cowherd boys) and *gopis* (cowherd girls) who were greatly devoted to him. Of all the gopis, Radha loved Krishna the most.

2. Barbara Stoller Miller, *The Gitagovinda of Jayadeva: Love Song of the Dark Lord* (Delhi, India: Motilal Banarsidass, 1984), pp. 88–89.

3. *Sati*, widows burning themselves on their dead husband's funeral pyres, is a practice that has to be seen in a historical context. Brave woman in medieval times chose to give up their lives rather than lose their honor to invading armies. Even in the absence of external aggressors, the custom continued as a means for widows to prove that they had lived as loyal wives. The government of India now bans the practice.

Chapter 11: Mirabai Marries Krishna

1. When the devotee grows in devotion (*bhakti*), there is absolute self-forgetfulness. This is called *bhava*. There are five kinds of bhavas in bhakti.

Shanta—where the devotee cultivates the devotion of a quiet joy and peace without being overly emotional. For example, Bhishma in the Mahabharatha is often pointed out as the ideal *Shanta Bhakta*.

Dasya—where the devotee cultivates devotion by being serviceful, considering himself as a servant of God, such as the devotion of Hanuman for Sri Rama.

Sakhya—where the devotee views God as an intimate friend, moving, sitting, eating, talking, and walking in the consciousness of the divine, such as the devotion of Arjuna for his friend and guru Krishna.

Vatsalya—where the devotee sees God as his or her own child, such as the devotion of the Mother Yashoda for her adopted child, Krishna.

Mathurya or kanta—where the devotee considers God as his or her lover. In Bhakti traditions, this is often considered the highest type, such as the love of Radha for Krishna, which Mirabai emulated.

2. *Arati* means "waving of lamps." When warriors went off to battle in medieval times, the women of the household waved lamps before them to bless them with light and the hope of victory.

3. Mirabai was called *kulnasi*, or "destructress of the clan," by her enemies, and she sang about her woes in many of her devotional songs. Her devotion to Krishna in a time torn by war and vendetta was seen as subversive to the state. Mira's singleminded and spontaneous *bhakti* (devotion) enabled her to live a life of love during a difficult time. For a comprehensive study of Mirabai's life and its significance in a cultural context, please read Parita Mukta's *Upholding the Common Life: The Community of Mirabai* (Delhi, India: OUP, 1994).

4. Vikramajita may have been the one who attempted to assassinate Mirabai, according to one version of the story (see A. J. Alston, *The Devotional Poems of Mirabai* [Delhi, India: Motilal Banarsidass, 1998], p. 5). Other versions mention that Rana tried to kill Mirabai, and we believe he had a stronger motivation to do so. In fact, in some of her compositions, Mira sings of how Rana tried to poison her and how she was saved miraculously by Krishna.

5. The Heat of Midnight Tears

    Listen, my friend, this road is the heart opening,
    Kissing his feet, resistance broken, tears all night.
    If we could reach the Lord through immersion in water,
    I would have asked to be born a fish in this life.
    If we could reach Him through nothing but berries
        and wild nuts
    Then surely the saints would have been monkeys when
        they came from the womb!
    If we could reach him by munching lettuce and dry leaves
    Then the goats would surely get to the Holy One before us!

If the worship of stone statues could bring us all the way,
I would have adored a granite mountain years ago.

Mirabai says, "The heat of midnight tears will bring you
to God."

From *Women in Praise of the Sacred: Forty-three Centuries of Spiritual Poetry by Women*, edited by Jane Hirschfield. (New York: Harper Collins, 1995).

Chapter 13: A Leap of Faith

1. Many sacred texts are replete with *vyas kutas*, or scriptural knot points, which often hide deep insights of the spiritual life. The sages did this to keep subtler points from casual or superficial readers who did not have the time or the patience to dig deeper.

2. During the medieval ages, the caste system rigidified into a pernicious social hierarchy, with the high castes treating the low castes poorly. The untouchables were people without a caste and hence were objects of derision.

3. *The Ramayana*, probably the world's oldest epic, describes the triumph of virtue over vice. The poem, written in *slokas* (verses), is divided into *sargas* (chapters), wherein a specific event is told. Sargas are grouped into *kandas* (books). The *Sundara Kanda* is the book in which Hanuman plays a prominent role. Valmiki, also known as *Adi Kavi* (literally, "the first poet"), was a great sage and the author of *The Ramayana*.

4. Some sources, such as Manipati's *Bhakta Vijaya*, attribute this story to Eknath.

Chapter 14: Vemana Mends His Ways

1. A note on this particular quality: Subjugation of the senses does not mean their mortification or suppression. One of the aims and ideals of Self-Realization Fellowship, the organization founded by Paramahansa Yogananda, may elucidate this quality: "To demon-

strate the superiority of mind over body, of soul over mind." The
story of Vemana proves how perilous it is for a man to disregard
this principle.

2. Later in his life, Vemana wrote:

"This I cannot do without"—
to think thus and be attached
and not be able to let things go
is the bondage of worldly life.
Know the immortal self and the Ultimate Self
You will not fall into the ocean of sin.

From Moorthy J. S. R. L. Narayana and Elliot Roberts, *Selected
Verses of Vemana* (New Delhi, India: Sahitya Akademi, 1995), p. 117.

Chapter 16: The Flawed Pot

1. Thy gifts to us mortals fulfill all our needs and yet run back
   to thee undiminished.

The river has its everyday work to do and hastens through
   fields and hamlets; yet its incessant stream winds toward the
   washing of thy feet.

The flower sweetens the air with its perfume; yet its last service is to offer itself to thee.

Thy worship does not impoverish the world.

From the words of the poet, men take what meanings please
   them; yet their last meaning points to thee.

From Rabindranath Tagore, *Gitanjali* (New York: Scribner Poetry,
1997), p. 93.

2. Namdev's last request was to be buried under the steps at the
entrance of the temple of Pandharpur, for he wanted his remains
to be perennially blessed by the feet of the devotees of Vithoba.
Translations of his poems can be found in *The Hindi Songs of
Namdev*, edited by Callewaert, Winand, and Mukund Lath (Delhi,
India: Motilal Banarsidass, 1989).

Chapter 17: Of Ledger Books and Liberation

1. One of the great sayings from the Bhagavad-Gita (2:50) is "Yogah karmasu kaushalam," translated as "Yoga is the art of proper action," from Yogananda's *God Talks with Arjuna: The Bhagavad-Gita*, p. 290.

Chapter 18: Milarepa Builds a Tower

1. We have omitted several episodes from Milarepa's life story for the purposes of this narrative. However, a full account of his life can be found in *Tibet's Great Yogi Milarepa: A Biography*, ed. W. Y. Evans-Wentz (New York: Oxford University Press, 1980).

2. These are Milarepa's own words from his online biography at *http://kagyu-asia.com/lineage/milarepa–life/milarepa5.html.* W. Y. Evans-Wentz, who wrote a noted biography on Milarepa, translated it as follows: "For I considered that it was my great evil-doing which debarred me from sharing in the ceremony, and I am pierced with remorse" (*Tibet's Great Yogi Milarepa: A Biography*, p. 110).

Chapter 19: The Governor's Last Day

1. The ancient *rishis* (sages) considered an ideal human life to be divided into four *ashramas* (stages). These were *brahmacharya*, the stage of celibacy and study; *grihastha*, the stage of fulfilling familial and societal duties; *vanaprastha*, the stage of retired life typically spent in a forest in order to cultivate detachment from material concerns; and *sannyasa*, the stage of complete renunciation and concentration on God.

2. The Upanashadic dictum—"dharmo rakshati rakshitah"—is one of the first principles taught to Hindu children at the start of their schooling. It means "Dharma protects those who protect Dharma."

Chapter 20: Namdev Feeds a Dog

1. Many commentators take actions such as Namdev's to be idol worship because they fail to understand the philosophical under-pinnings. In the ultimate sense, Hinduism teaches that God is One, formless, and beyond all qualities. Therefore, the Lord can be dif-

ficult to approach, particularly for the beginner on the spiritual path. To better relate to his Creator, the Hindu prays to a particular aspect of the Unmanifested Absolute that is dear to him: Siva, Vishnu, Kali, Durga, and so on. As the devotee advances spiritually, he may outgrow the need to pray to a personal god. The temple rituals of India have a deep spiritual purpose—to bring an awareness of God into every thought and action. The seeker who devoutly performs these rituals with an understanding of their symbolic meanings achieves mental purification and redemption. The purposes behind both these methods are to bring the awareness of God into every thought and act.

Chapter 21: Ramanuja Disobeys His Guru

1. In his later years, Ramanuja propounded a philosophy called *Vishista Advaita* (qualified nondualism), a modification of Adi Sankara's *Advaita* philosophy.

Advaita claims that God alone exists; for many this statement was a negation of creation as we perceive it. Ramanuja appreciated the conclusions of Advaita, but felt they were too abstract and grand to be of practical use to worldly men. He agreed that God is the sole cause and underlying reality, but also added that all creatures and everything in creation exist as different manifestations of that one God. Thus was born a philosophy that reconciled Advaita's strict nondualism with our need to live and work in this world. Ramanuja's concern for the common man is wonderfully reflected in his major philosophical treatises.

2. "That which is night (of slumber) to all creatures is (luminous) wakefulness to the man of self-mastery. And what is wakefulness to ordinary man, that is night (a time for slumber) to the divinely perceptive sage" (*God Talks with Arjuna: The Bhagavad-Gita*, p. 317). Buddhist scriptures echo this thought: "Those who think the unreal is real and see the real as unreal do not reach the real, being in the realm of false thinking. Those who know the real is real and

see the unreal as unreal arrive at the real, being in the realm of accurate thought"(*Dhammapada: The Sayings of Buddha*, p. 10).

3. Ancient India's society had four divisions called *varnas* (literally, "color"), now known as castes. Just as all the colors together make one white light, the various castes were intended to work as one to produce a complete and harmonious society. Those of the Brahmin varna were scholars and teachers; the Kshatriyas were rulers and warriors; the Vaishyas were businessmen and artists; and the Sudras were farmers and artisans. Castes were not rigid distinctions originally but merely a way to connote one's position in life. For example, a child born to a father who was a Sudra could take up the priestly duties of a Brahmin. It was not until later on that the caste system became rigidified and oppressive.

4. *Om Namo Narayanaya* means "I bow to Lord Narayana." Narayana is conceived as the Supreme Godhead beyond creation. Each of these Sanskrit words is composed of sacred syllables that have many esoteric meanings.

5. Ramanuja was forgiven by his guru, and he went on to become the head of the Mutt (monastery) at Srirangam. His act that day on the *gopurams* had a ripple effect and ultimately led to many inspired reformations of Hinduism.

Chapter 22: Tulsidas Runs Off to His Wife

1. Many versions of this story have Tulsidas grabbing a snake, mistaking it for a vine. The authors believe that this is symbolic of the rising *kundalini* and Tulsidas's spiritual ascent from this point onward. Yoga treatises define the kundalini as the coiled up sexual energy at the base of the spine that can be transmuted into regenerative spinal currents.

2. "Brooding on sense objects causes attachment to them. Attachment breeds craving; craving breeds anger. Anger breeds delusion; delusion breeds loss of memory (of the Self). Loss of

right memory causes decay of the discriminating faculty. From decay of discrimination, annihilation (of the spiritual life) follows." (*God Talks with Arjuna: The Bhagavad-Gita*, p. 307).

Chapter 23: The Might of the Mighty

1. Islamic ruler.

2. "Sanatana Dharma" means "Age-old, or Eternal, Righteousness," which was the original name of Hinduism.

3. Gopanna's building a temple was significant. In Indian culture, temples traditionally were not only houses of worship but were philanthropic institutions, places for the performances of the arts, and centers for communal gatherings and kinship.

4. Lakshmana was the younger brother of Lord Rama. In *The Ramayana*, Lakshmana accompanied Rama through his many tests and served him unflinchingly. They demonstrated the highest form of brotherly love.

5. After Gopanna's struggles, he was called "Bhadrachala Ramadasu" or "Rama's servant from Bhadrachalam." The objects and places involved in the narrative—the temple in Bhadrachalam; the prison cell in Golconda Fort; the "fingernail" drawing of Sri Rama; the gold and jewels given to *Nizam* Tanashah—have been preserved and are considered sacred objects. Tanashah's family made yearly offerings to the temple at Bhadrachalam for many generations. The government of Andhra Pradesh now continues that tradition.

Chapter 24: Upasena's Last Breath

1. Upasena's reference to chaff is an analogy to the soul that is like grain encased in the husk of the body.

Chapter 25: Adi Sankara and the Chandala

1. *Adi* means "first." Sankara was so called because he was the first in an ecclesiastical line. *Chandala* is a person who is an untouchable,

someone who is beyond even the pale of the caste system and hence, for the prejudiced people of eighth-century India, a despicable man.

2. The Upanishads are sacred and esoteric treatises in Sanskrit composed by ancient seers. There are eighteen Upanishads.

3. Sankara's system of philosophy known as *Advaita* (nonduality) taught that there is only one Reality as Absolute Consciousness and that we perceive this One Reality as multifarious due to the cosmic delusion of maya. In this instance, because he found himself failing to live up to his own teachings, the great teacher was deeply troubled.

Chapter 26: Nandanar Waits for Lord Nataraja

1. Nataraja is a form of Lord Siva as the great Cosmic Dancer of Bliss.

2. The four most revered Nayanar saints (worshipers of Siva) of South India—Appar, Sundarar, Sambandar, and Manikkavachar—worshiped at the Nataraja temple at Chidambaram and breathed their last breaths there. Their images are placed at the four *gopuram* entrances of the temple.

3. The mridangam is an Indian percussion instrument used in classical music and in temple services.

4. *Darshan* means "holy sight" of God or a saint that uplifts and inspires.

5. Nandanar was called "Thiru Nalai Povar" Nayanar by his admirers, or the "I'm going (to Chidambaram) tomorrow" saint.

6. The Nataraja statue at Chidambaram is called the "Ananda Tandava" pose, or the pose of the blissful dance.

SELECT BIBLIOGRAPHY

Alston, A. J. *The Devotional Poems of Mirabai*. Delhi, India: Motilal Banarsidass, 1998.

Augustine, St. *Confessions*. New York: Vintage Books, 1998.

Bamzai, Kaul P. N. *Forerunner of Medieval Mystics*. Kashmir, India: Koshur Samachar, 2000.

Cleary, Thomas. *Dhammapada: The Sayings of Buddha*. New York: Bantam Wisdom Editions, 1995.

Das, G. N. *Couplets from Kabir*. Delhi: Motilal Banarsidass, 1991.

Dhammapada. Translated from the Pali by P. Lal. New York: Noonday Press, 1967.

Gangopadhyay, Sunil. *Those Days*. Translated by Aruna Chakravarti. New Delhi, India: Penguin Books, 1997.

Housden, Roger. *Sacred America*. New York: Simon & Schuster, 1999.

Khanolkar, Savitribai. *Saints of Maharashtra*. Bombay, India: Bharatiya Vidya Bhavan, 1978.

Mahipati. *Bhaktavijaya: Stories of Indian Saints*. Translated by Justin Abbott and Nahar Godbole. Delhi: Motilal Banarsidass, 1999.

Miller, Barbara Stoler. *The Gitagovinda of Jayadeva: Love Song of the Dark Lord*. Delhi, India: Motilal Banarsidass, 1984.

Mukta, Parita. *Upholding the Common Life: The Community of Mirabai*. Delhi, India: Oxford University Press, 1994.

Murcott, Susan. *The First Buddhist Women: Translations and Commentary on the Therigatha*. Berkley, Calif.: Parallax Press, 1991.

Narayana, Moorthy J. S. R. L., and Roberts, Elliot. *Selected Verses of Vemana*. New Delhi, India: Sahitya Akademi, 1995.

Raghukumar, T. *Bhakta Nandanar*. Tirupati, India: Tirumala Tirupati Devasthanam, 1990.

Rajagopalachari. C. *The Mahabharata*. Mumbai, India: Siddhi Printers, 1999.

Sangamesam, M. *Tulsidas*. Tirupati, India: Tirumala Tirupati Devasthanam, 1990.

Shakespeare, William. *Hamlet*. Edited by Stephen Orgel. New York: Penguin Putnam, 2001.

————. *The Merchant of Venice*. Edited by Stephen Orgel. New York: Penguin Putnam, 2001.

Sivananda, Swami. *Lives of the Saints*. Vols. I & II. Rishikesh, India: The Sivananda Publication League, 1947.

Strong, John S. *The Legend and Cult of Upagupta*. Princeton, N.J.: Princeton University Press, 1992.

Tagore, Rabindranath. *Gitanjali*. New York: Scribner Poetry, 1997.

The Holy Bible. Wheaton, Ill.: Tyndale House Publishers, 1976.

The Holy Quran. Translated by Maulana Muhammad Ali. Columbus, Ohio: Ahmadiyyah Anjuman Isha'at Islam Lahore, Inc., 1991.

Tibet's Great Yogi Milarepa: A Biography from the Tibetan. Edited by W. Y. Evans-Wentz. New York: Oxford University Press, 1980.

Vivekananda, Swami. *The Complete Works of Swami Vivekananda*. Calcutta, India: Advaita Ashrama, 1970.

Women in Praise of the Sacred: Forty-three Centuries of Spiritual Poetry by Women. Edited by Jane Hirschfield. New York: Harper Collins, 1994.

Yogananda, Paramahansa. *Autobiography of a Yogi.* Los Angeles: Self-Realization Fellowship, 1975.

———. *God Talks with Arjuna: The Bhagavad-Gita.* Los Angeles: Self-Realization Fellowship, 1996.

———. *Man's Eternal Quest.* Los Angeles: Self-Realization Fellowship, 1975.

Zubko, Andy. *Treasury of Spiritual Wisdom.* San Diego: Blue Dove Press, 1998.

CREDITS

All excerpts from Paramahansa Yogananda's interpretation of the Bhagavad Gita come from *God Talks with Arjuna: The Bhagavad Gita* by Paramahansa Yogananda (Los Angeles, Calif.: Self-Realization Fellowship, 1995). Used with permission.

The selections from Jayadeva's *Gitagovinda* on pages 57–58 is taken from *Gitagovinda by Jayadeva,* translated by Barbara Stoler Miller (Delhi, India: Motilal Banarsidas, 1984). Pages 88–89. Used with permission.

"In the Valley of Sorrow," which serves as the epigraph for "Nandanar Waits for Lord Natajara" on page 164, is taken from *Cosmic Chants* by Paramahansa Yogananda (Los Angeles, Calif.: Self-Realization Fellowship, 1995), p. 18. Used with permission.

The poem "Let Them Jeer or Cheer Me" by Lallashwari, which appears on page 179 of the endnotes, was translated by P. N. Kaul Bamzai and is taken from *Forerunner of Medieval Mystics* (Kashmir, India: Koshur Samachar, 2002), p. 2. Used with permission.

"Samsara," by Vemana, which appears on page 183 of the endnotes, is taken from *The Selected Verses of Vemana* by J. S. R. Narayana Moorthy and Elliot Roberts (New Delhi, India: Sahitya Akademi, 1995), p. 117. Used with permission.

The poem by Rabindranath Tagore that appears on page 183 of the endnotes comes from *Gitanjali* (New York, N.Y.: Simon & Schuster, 1944; Kolakata, India: Visva-Bharati), Used with permission.